I want to thank all those that helped me aspire to putting my book out there. All the mediums in these pages that were able to validate life beyond here. To Jeannie thank you for pushing me to get this finished and for being my biggest fan, reading this and letting me know just how much you loved it. To Rocky for giving me the idea and the courage to share our story. To all those that have been supportive of me and my work I appreciate you.

I want to thank my mom for always believing in me and telling me I'm a good writer. To my Aunt Sharon for always helping me out of a jam

To all those Twin Flames out there I feel for you. Know that what you're feeling is real and our path is never easy. To those that have lost loved ones, I hope this has taught you that you will see them again.

This is a story about Loss and how Love remains.

Chapter 1: The Meeting

I was always searching for a love I had dreamt about all my life. To love and be loved. I had relationships but none had given me that feeling of completeness that I had always longed for. However, I was at the time in my life when I never thought I would discover that kind of relationship and was just about to give up on finding that special someone when I met him. On May 26, 2011 while looking through an acquaintance's Facebook page I found this handsome man. Who was playfully commenting on the same post I was. I never thought I stood a chance but I messaged him anyway. I inquired "Are you really 66?" It was the age he had put on his profile. Little to my surprise I received a response. "I look good for 66 rights?" Laughing inside I thought to myself there is no way this beautiful man is 66. I replied "those must not be recent pictures. Seriously?? Or did you just put that? I have met people that put up old pictures and look nothing like they do now so that's why I ask. It says you were born in 1945!" He said "I just put that. My attempt at humor. The pictures are new" Right away I felt a rush. I didn't want to feel this way about this man. He looked like a heartbreaker. But I couldn't help but be intrigued and wonder who he was? I replied "Ha well funny I suppose!! Alright then you're a hot 66 yr. old!" This was my attempt at making him laugh and giving him a compliment all at the same time. My messages lit up, it read "I like that at 66 I can get a compliment ha" I think this guy was getting to me too much, keep your distance I thought to myself. But I couldn't help it this man already had a hold on me and I didn't know how or why all I knew is that I was in trouble. I read the message fast and replied quickly "I gave you one I said you were hot! Oh Never mind I reread that you guys and your gangster talk ha ha. Yes you can, I like to give compliments when they are deserved" and to me that was an understatement. But why was this guy interested in me?? He could have anyone he wanted right? The conversation went on like that for a while. Both of us playing with each other and flirting. We seemed to get along really well. Then I got my first compliment from him " yea you are very attractive and we do watch a lot of the same TV shows"

I think to myself, how can a man that looks like this think that I am very attractive? I rebutted "Well thank you, coming from you that's a nice compliment. Yea when I get to watch them" He didn't fully get what I meant so I had to come out and say it " Um because your hot so coming from a hot guy that's a good compliment" Whew I don't know how I got up the courage to say that to him then he made me smile with the words. "Well aren't you charming? Thank you. I'm blushing, you made my day. Thanks. Ummmm LOL I forgot what I was gonna say" No way I thought, he has to get compliments like this all the time. We talked for a bit longer. I have to say, that night I went home with him on my mind. Wondering about him. Hoping this could lead somewhere. I don't know why but I felt I already knew him and couldn't help but like him. I felt my heart beat fast at just the thought of him. The next morning I got a message "You made quite the impression yesterday. Figured I'd say, "Good Morning Beautiful" And now I was hooked.

We began to talk all day every day and I instantly fell in love with him. It was like I had finally found the other half of my soul. It was this beautiful proud Native American man with this intensity that could not be tamed. However, our situation was going to be difficult. He was honest with me and explained that because of self-defense gone wrong, he was in prison. He had kind of a hard life and was paying the price. Normally this would be a deal breaker for me and I would turn away. For some reason with him I didn't care. My heart wanted what it wanted. I couldn't ignore this deep connection or the love that filled my existence. My thought process was people make mistakes and from the story he told me he was treated unfairly. Also, that he is human just as I am and that everyone is capable of making bad decisions. I couldn't help but feel empathy and compassion for him. I wanted to be there for him. I wanted to comfort and love him. It didn't matter the circumstances I couldn't let him go. We just had this amazing connection that I had never experienced with anyone else before in my life. Somehow I felt like he completed me. That he was the man I had dreamed about so many times before. When we couldn't talk or text I felt like I was going crazy. It was like a piece of me was missing. I woke up to a "Good Morning Beautiful Baby Girl" message every day. We never went to sleep without saying goodnight. We spoke for hours on the phone the longest being 7 and

3

that was an all-time record. Sure we had our ups and downs with miscommunication but who doesn't?   We were always posting cute stuff on Facebook and everyone thought we were so adorable and began to admire our love. The way he spoke to me was with love. I could tell he was guarded but he wanted to let me in and in a short amount of time he did. We decided to make it official on July 6, 2011. He used to tell me that "We was written in the stars Baby Girl" and I would tell him he was the ying to my yang. Little did we know our destiny was tied together in a way neither of us could've ever imagined? The distance didn't matter we were in love and we hadn't even met yet. He would send me beautiful cards and we even wrote from time to time. Here is an example of his love for me on a masterpiece with wolves and a dream catcher: Little did I know that the wolves would have even a deeper meaning later on but that wolves are symbolic of choosing a mate for life.

"Baby girl, I wanted to write you a little some time to let you know I think of you and care for you deeply. I can't wait for visiting and the moment I get out to show you just how special I can make you feel. F-Baby girl to feel your loving arms around me and taste your lips on mine. I can't wait to hold your beautiful face in my hands as I kiss you and watch your eye's fill with a gaze of lust and love. I tell you Baby girl, I can't wait to love on you for all of the hours we have missed to act out all of the fantasy's we talked about. I want badly to kiss and lick. To kiss on ur neck that special way I do, and with that same kiss I want to kiss you in all the spots my mind has kissed. I swear I can make you feel so amazing and let you realize you're the most luckiest woman in the world. I promise you that. I love kissing your eyes and tasting your tears. Soul mates cherish each other's feelings and believe in each other's dreams. Cherishing, believing and treasuring you. Our destiny is in the stars. Let's make this Happen! Love me without conditions and I'll make you the luckiest woman and more envied...Always Daddy"

 I felt like my heart had found a home. Finally the weekend I would meet him face to face arrived. It was first weekend in August. I rented a car and began my journey that would become a habit. I got lost and I drove all night but he stayed on the phone with me to keep me awake. We both only got an hour of sleep that night. The whole experience was different for me. It was something I had never done nor wanted to do, but that didn't matter. My love for him was so strong I would do just about anything. He had broken down all my walls. When I saw him walk in my heart skipped a beat. When our eyes met I knew I only wanted this man forever. I can't explain fully what I felt but I knew that it was special. We talked like we had known each other forever. He made me blush and I made him smile. I only thought I had experienced love before. But this was all unfamiliar territory. I never expected to feel this way. One of the hardest things I ever had to do was walk away on Sunday when it was time for me to leave. I felt a pull at my heart. It was as if something was missing. I couldn't stand to be away from him and couldn't wait till the day we could finally be together. Driving home he was in my ear. To hear him say I was even more beautiful in person lit up my smile. He made me feel so attractive and so loved. We were going to be beasts on the battlefield of love never letting anything come between us. No one had ever stuck by him for the whole time and I couldn't let him down. As he would say we were forming R&R love. A special bond unlike any other. We felt this pull towards each other and knew that what we had was not of this world but we didn't realize exactly what was going on. However he sent me these words, I share these things to give you an idea just how special he and our love was:

My Beautiful Dream Girl...I just wanted to take some time out of my life and try to show you I care plus I do cherish you. Baby girl you're a truly amazing woman. I am so lucky and blessed to have and hold the attention of a Gorgeous Goddess.! Thank you for smiling and looking at me. Most of all I appreciate your love and how you love me. I want you to know you never merely cross my mind, you always come and stay a while, long enough to lift my spirits, warm my heart and make me smile. I hope you have a great day Baby Girl. Believe and know I deeply love you and need you. Always thinking of my Dream Girl respectfully and lovingly. Rocky xoxox

These kind of notes always tugged at my heartstrings. Our love was so deep….Divine! When our lifeline, the phone he would use, wasn't available anymore we began to write. I wrote him every single day. Sometimes more than one letter a day. It was the only way to ease the emptiness I felt from not hearing his voice. I did still hear his voice from time to time but it was hard adjusting to it not being all day every day. It was hard to breathe. The above was only a taste of the kind of letters we wrote to each other I have many more filled with immense love. I sent him a story I had read about this old couple always putting the acronym SHMILY all over the house. Written in sugar on the table, on the toilet paper. Everywhere they knew the other would find it. No one their whole life knew what this meant not even the grandchildren. Till the wife died and the husband said at the funeral that SHMILY meant "See How Much I Love You". We were both touched by the story and decided to adopt that tradition. Pretty soon it was on every letter and later on it was on everything we could find. We used to say that we were going to notebook it, meaning that we were going to exit this life together just like in the movie. We seemed to talk about that and what he would do if anything happened to me. Like if our souls knew something we didn't. I still went to see him about every other weekend. Our visits were filled with as much love as possible. I think others looked at us differently and we almost got in trouble a couple of times but we didn't care. We were in love and showed our affection. He would stroke my hair and look into my eyes. He just made me feel like a woman who was deeply cared about. We would fantasize about when we could be together and how we were going to live our life. We had many dreams of our future. As he would say:

Baby girl....Love is that mysterious capacity which enables two persons in the most intimate communion to remain themselves. In their love they truly become themselves. The sign of true love is what it makes of the lovers. In love each realizes more fully the self they have been seeking through their beloved. The person they always knew they was now more given in the relationship is the presence of the other to oneself. That is all...But it is in comparably significant. I love how you love me and I love how you make me feel about me being me. SHMILY. I love and need you girl.

Someday you will realize
How the day just brightens every
Moment you appear so beautifully
In my mind's eye but
Lately every moment

You do appear you're so much more beautiful than before

The letters went on like that until it was time for him to be released but something was messed up in the system so he had to go to court. I made sure I was there although I think he thought I wouldn't show up. During all of this time I had gotten my own place because I had been living with my mother. But I wanted my love to come home to a place of peace and wanted us to be together because I couldn't stand being apart anymore. The case was an error so was dismissed and he was able to come home with me. When he walked out I jumped into his arms. It felt so good for him to hold me. We moved into our house together on Oct 8, 2011...but at first all that we had was a couch. We slept on it that night and I felt the magic of us being one. I had never felt the way he made me feel. It was as if our souls had merged...It was Intense and exciting. I never felt so much love. I knew I wanted to be in his arms forever. Lying on his chest listening to his heart, I was finally home for good.

He continued to show his love to me through his words. I felt every ounce of feeling he put into his letters. His words continued to touch me and so I want to share because in order for you to understand how he truly was you need to hear his wisdom and love.

Happy Anniversary my loyal and devoted love

I hope and want you to remember us on our first steps together to reach the thing and place people call utopia. At first I found myself slowing the pace not really caring if I got there or not. My utopia is just being with you no matter where we are. Your truly amazing to me your smile, eyes and laughter is equivalent to birds singing me awake in the freshest of mornings, the breath taking dazzlement of a clear night sky as magical stars shoot forth burst of joys lights and calming sounds of the most amazingly beautiful waterfall you can imagine, but I must tell you my love that you have a completely different effect on me. Tho your smile, eyes and laughter make me remember the description I said above. You are truly an amazing woman. Your smile dazzles me and always puts me in a better mood and your laughter calms my body and soul. Truly you do! You're so very beautiful and damn sexy baby girl!! Believe it you really are. I have come to a

7

realization that astounds me yet I welcome ...its kind of weird that says "is not the lite that soothes your spirit the very wood that was hollowed with knives?" "The deeper that sorrow carves into your being the more joy you can contain" I like to think I am in much more control of my emotions yet you do seem to unintentionally bring me sorrow. Like when you leave or just at times throughout the day when I miss you. "And so when you are joyous look deep into your heart & soul and you shall find it is only that which has given you sorrow that is giving you joy" Do you feel me? Does that make sense to you? "When you are sorrowful look again in your heart and you shall see that in truth you are weeping for that which has been your delight" Some people say joy is greater than sorrow, others say "sorrow is greater." Yet Baby girl they are inseparable. My feelings for you have made me realize this "together they come and when one sits alone with you at your board, remember that the other is asleep upon your bed. And I can only now except the facts and enjoy you when we are together for that is when I'm at my happiest, yet our memories and time together when recalled keeps the fluid of sorrow at bay. You feel my Baby girl? Our love is eye opening and deep it brings me understanding when I do introspections. It's funny the souls is oftentimes a battlefield, upon which your reason & your judgment wage war against your passion and your appetite. Yet we both know it's the forces of the enemy that is cunning and diabolical in its plan to separate us. It's in the form of people and world circumstances that declared war on our love and want to be together. They make our love a battlefield that we as one must come to its defense and be the battlefield beasts for R&R love! For me my reason to possess passion is you. And so my passion is now directed with reason making you my soul's peacemaker. I shall await my better half with arms extended and full intentions to prevail in our struggle. LOL Just kinda started ranting huh. Let me Focus. SHMILY. A true beast on the battlefield defending R&R! I hope you understand what I'm telling you. Happy Anniversary Baby Girl. I can't remember the whole thing tho now I wish I tried but when I think of it I think of you. I'm sure you're familiar with it: "You may not be her first, her last or her only. She loved before she will love again but if she loves you now what else matters? She may not be thinking of you every second of the day but she will give you a part of her, she knows you can break her heart. Don't hurt her, don't change her, don't analyze her and don't expect more than she

8

can give." I like that kinda wish I knew the whole thing. Yet I love you just the way you are. You know what other song makes me smile & just imagine you? Bob Marley. Is this love...yet I only remember: I wanna love you & treat you right, I wanna love you every day and every night. We'll be together with a roof right over our head. That's all I know baby girl. You know what blew me for a loop? I'll tell you...I heard that Bruno mars song...I'm not sure what to do about it? And you're right it says what I say to you. So I should try to buy it and make it yours. Yet as you know it's all how I see you. And I said it to you first. Nevertheless your eyes do make it seem like the stars aren't shining. You're so beautiful and I tell you as much as I can because I truly believe it. I know when I compliment you, you don't believe me and I find it sad you don't see anything I see. But one day you will. "When I see your face there's not a thing that I would change because you're amazing just the way you are" Your truly perfect Baby Girl and I do love you just the way you are. Happy Anniversary my Gorgeous Goddess...Remember I'm always thinking of you & loving how you love me...Your Indian and Daddy...R&R Battlefield Beast of Love..SHMILY...I do Appreciate your loyalty and devoted love...I love and need you Baby girl!

His love spoke to me and I loved him just as deeply as he loved me. We just couldn't help it our hearts were tied together. Our meeting and love destined.

With all love stories there are always ups and downs at one time or another. He struggled with himself over a lot of things about his past. I tried to ease the pain. But sometimes I think it was too much for him to bear. When this happens with someone we love we often have to think "what made them this way" this is why I had patience for things even when he did to try run away. We did love each other deeply but it wasn't something he was used to. He wasn't used to the love he felt and the love I showed him. I think in a way it was scary. And in the future I would grow to understand this more. We were married on November 4, 2011. It was one of the most amazing days of my life as I looked into his eyes vowing to love him forever my eyes filled with tears of happiness. I had this feeling of knowing that I never wanted anyone else I just wanted him and only him forever. Although no one but my friend who was the witness knew what we were doing it didn't matter. The only reason it was kept a secret was because we had planned to have a real wedding one day. After the ceremony we went to eat and then came home. He would tell me "Baby girl did we elope?" I would laugh and say "we sure did." It was cute to us.

From that day on we celebrated two anniversaries instead of just one. One on the 4th and on on the 6th of each month. We would always give each other cards or do something special to remind each other just how one of a kind our love was. When we loved it was like no one in the world mattered. One of the cards he gave me on our anniversary:

Because I love you very much

Beautiful Loyal & Loving Wife...Happy Anniversary
I have no words to express the depths of how you affect me...the very definition of R&R love is just now being formed. So I am limited on my knowledge...yet I can say that I will not use hollow words to express my love for you....I will fill the words with my soul and punctuate my statements with my actions!!! I love you so deeply and with every fiber of my being...You're all I want and need in this world. You're the most amazing woman I have met. You're every essence of Beauty! I love how you love me Baby girl. Thank you for being yourself and my truest gift. Without you love wouldn't mean shit. I live for you. Your truly amazing and so beautiful, sexy gorgeous and mine!

You're Daddy, friend, lover, hubby, soul mate, your truest companion, your beast on the battlefield!!

Our love continued. I share the letters to put you in the experience of love that we felt. Also so that u can understand the kind of person Rocky is and the love he felt for me.

"My Loyal & Loving Dream girl"

My days are so much brighter now that we have a few pictures. God you're so beautiful baby girl and I love to stare at the picture of us together. I must say we are the greatest looking couple this world has *ever laid eyes on. Yet 75% of the beauty comes from you. You make us look fantastic. F*** you have no idea just how much I love you. Baby girl the deepest and greatest love you can ever imagine is possibly only a microscopic fraction of what I feel for you. MWAH! I'm so happy I married your flat footed A**. I truly do love us. I know from here on out its nothing but love, we will live happy lives, deeply in love, and for eternity and beyond! I always told myself and I believe you can never know or truly trust a person until you see how they behave in other situations. And I always said if I can find a girl that can and will love me at my worst and stay faithful and loyal to me while I'm away I'd love her forever. And until now, no one has ever been stuck at my side through thick and thin. So far only you have shown me and stuck with me, only you have took care of me in my greatest time of need and show me love. F*** I love you Baby girl! I'm sure you'll stick this ride out and become my only love that has truly stuck by me through thick and thin. I truly want nothing more than to spend the rest of my life with you. I believe your right it's the trials and tribulations that make things clearer yet it's never too late. You need to have hard times...it's kind of weird but it's as if the hard times adds a value to our relationship. As if we are earning a right to possess the special kind of R&R love we want. Make sense? When something is hard to possess and obtain yet we fight and struggle until we do possess the harder the fight the deeper our sentiment for the acquired target. No matter what anyone says the feelings for the object are more than anyone can understand. "You don't know what I've been through to get and keep his/her love I'm never giving up I'm never giving up!" I want to show you my love how much I truly adore you, how amazing you are to me. I want to love you and treat you right Baby girl. Show you who I am. And how I can love you and care for you more than anyone else. I truly hope you know & believe that. Please know that I love you. I love you deeply Baby girl*

Always you're Daddy,
Rocky

Chapter 2: Turn of Events

Once we were married we both knew we wanted to add to our family...we wanted a baby. So I made an appointment to have my birth control removed. We were in love and what better way to bring a child into the world...It seemed like I got pregnant because I would throw up in the mornings and would end up calling into work. We started to have some struggles and stress. He began acting differently. There are some things I won't go into here...I had taken pregnancy tests and they came back negative. Which I know if they are taken too early they will. Then one day I had a tremendous pain and a ton of blood. It felt as If I had a miscarriage. I never went to the doctor to confirm it but a woman knows her body. I think all the stress and stuff that was going on was just too much. Little did I know I would understand all of this later and get answers.

As he continued to struggle with certain things in his life. He had let people into his life that weren't good for him. I learned later that we had something so special that the dark would continue to try and break us up...Due to this, our relationship became challenging at times. I always worried about him when he was away and become very intuitive when it came to him. I somehow knew when he was going to call me or something of that nature. If there was going to be a problem I somehow knew before there ever was. This would amaze him sometimes. We never knew that there could be something behind all this connection and intuitiveness towards each other. He would make my lunch for work and always include a note saying how beautiful he thought I was or how much he loved me. I would constantly come home to a clean house. He would spoil me after a long day at work with a massage or just love on me. He wanted to feel like I needed him. He would put the plates on the top shelf just so I had to ask for his help. When I was sick he would pick me up and bring me to the couch in living room, then he would make me soup. We enjoyed cuddling up on the couch watching movies. When I would be in the shower he would poke his head in through the curtain and give me a kiss as he watched me like I was the only girl in the world. When he took showers I would just stare at his beauty I wanted to burn that image into my mind. We would go on hikes and he would

12

help me up the mountain either by carrying me or moving the branches. I am going to mention right now that I have a son who is not his biological son. However, to him my son was his own. They were always playing together and doing manly things it was wonderful to watch them. Rocky taught my son a lot. We all made a trip to Ventura beach and made some wonderful memories. I remember when Rocky and I went to Magic Mountain for Fright fest. He laughed at me as I rode the roller coasters and when we passed someone who was dressed up he held me by my belt in front of them because it cracked him up to see me scream. We went to Vegas to try and win the rent, silly I know, when we didn't have a place to sleep I crawled in his lap in the car and felt so comfortable. It felt good to be held in this way. For my birthday in February he made me a wedding ring out of string that said R&R Love. It was beautiful and so special because he created it.

He made me feel so loved. He would stroke my hair and kiss me tenderly. I felt butterflies every time our lips touched and when we made love I was filled with the overpowering feeling of being in love. And our souls connecting as one. It was magic. We laughed constantly and knew he would bring a smile to my face. I could count on him to make me feel like a beautiful woman. He would tell me "Baby girl I am so glad we are here together and I am not out getting into trouble" I knew he wanted a new life although I also knew it was hard for him. What we had was not of earth. My love for him grew every day although I wasn't sure how it could grow any more. I felt like I would die without him. I never wanted to imagine a life that didn't contain him and us. I guess that's why I always worried about him. As if I knew deep down that one day I could lose him.

Things seemed to change when he began to hang with people that would get him into trouble. I didn't understand how people that supposedly loved him and knew he wanted to have a straight happy life could bring him down just because that is where they wanted to be. I soon realized there was nothing I could do but love him through it and try to help him in any way I could after all our Vows said "for better or worse." But I realized that I didn't need Vows to be there for him through thick and thin. Sometimes it was as if he was not himself. There were times I did not recognize him. I will go into more detail later. But let's just say it was hard. Very hard. It was a struggle to see someone you love so deeply spiral downhill and to be stuck in this tornado of destruction and all the things he had promised go right along with it. The happy life gone. Slipping through my fingers and his promises he made me broken. He was not strong enough to fight against the outside forces that tried to tear us apart and he began to start saying to me Death before I dishonor my loyal and loving wife. He gave in and this caused us much grief and pain in our relationship. More than many would understand or could comprehend. He didn't want help because he didn't feel he had a problem. But he did. The times when I did not recognize him were the times of immense pain for me. I just wanted to save him, but at times it seemed like he was beyond my help. I had no choice I would do anything he asked of me just because I loved him, and it was a love like no other. I couldn't bear to see him this way and yet I couldn't bear to tear myself apart from him. Things had finally hit a boiling point and I think a lot of it was deep inside he knew he was out of control and he didn't want me in the cross hairs of his destruction anymore. So he decided to leave for a while. One night he had me drive him to a family member's house because he had some things he needed to do. However, something was off. The whole time we drove he wasn't really himself. When he kissed me and tried to say goodbye we couldn't leave each other at first. It was like a part of him didn't want to go. I wish that he would've listened to that good part of him. I didn't want to let him go because I had a bad feeling I would never see him again. My heart ached and I had this sickness fill me inside that things were going to change. That something awful was going to happen. When I pulled away I cried because I knew something was wrong. Somehow I felt that was the last time we would kiss or hug or that he would stroke my hair and look into my eyes. I still can't explain how I knew that something was terribly wrong. I tried to follow him just to know where he was because he had me drop him off in a field. But it was like he disappeared into the dusk.

The following week was stressful for me. It was a roller coaster ride. Lots of highs and lows. He would call me and act as himself then the next day would act totally different. It was like his dark side was coming out but I know that it was because of who he was at the time and where he was. He was under some bad influences that he was not strong enough to fight. He was altered by things he shouldn't have been doing. I felt that he was torn. I knew he loved me deeply but I didn't fully understand what was going on. It was like something else had taken him over. What had happened to my husband? My depression grew as I missed him and worried about him. I am going to share something very hard here because I feel that it is a part of the story that needs to be told. It goes along with the hardship. Rocky had this hold on me; I had never acted as crazy in my life as when he would leave....because I felt as If I could not breathe....he would run away a lot. Later on I began to understand but at the time it just broke my heart. I was in so much pain. Pain that I could not comprehend or bare. I had just started taking antidepressants. One night on May 25th he called me, not himself yet again. He said something to try and hurt me, and it cut deep! I didn't know why he was saying these things except for that he was struggling with the demons inside himself. I did not recognize who he was or what he was saying. I guess between him saying this and hurting me the deepest hurt I had ever felt and the fact that I had just started a new medication, I began to spiral myself. Not recognizing what I was doing or even who I was. I began taking pain pills that I had for my back which I had hurt a few months before. I could not control my actions I just knew that I wanted the pain to end. I took another antidepressant without realizing it trying to help myself. It caused me to spiral even more. Before I knew it I had taken many pain pills. I remember vaguely calling and leaving a goodbye message on a phone for Rocky. Saying how much I loved him. I then realized what was happening to me and called a friend for help. In the meantime Rocky called back all of a sudden being his loving self who was worried about me. Trying to help me and apologizing. When my friend got there she tried to help but she was a nurse and realized my blood pressure was way too low. So she had to call the ambulance. I only remember bits and pieces of that night. I remember drinking the charcoal and then being rolled into a room. I remember Rocky calling a few times to see how I was and talking to me. Telling me how sorry he was, and how bad he felt. How he never wanted anything to happen to me. He told me at that moment that things would change. He was ready for them to change. They sent me to the mental ward the next day and I had to talk to them and tell them it was an accident and felt it was a reaction to my new antidepressants as well which Prozac was. They realized that it was just a horrible mistake and that I could go home. Rocky kept calling sometimes acting normal and sometimes not. He said he was coming to pick me up as soon as someone could take him to my car, but he never showed up. The security guard was nice enough to take me home as I had no one else to call. When I got home I was upset, because he had promised things would be different. It was at this time where I felt I was going to give him an ultimatum that I was just done. I had to be. He was dragging me down with him and I was drowning. No matter how much I loved him I could not fight for our love alone. I knew he loved me and I loved him with all my heart but he had to change and want to get some sort of help in order for this to continue. We spoke that afternoon when I got home and he was sort of himself but not really. He said that he would come home and we would talk about it.

He had made the decision to come home on May 26th, 2012 and as far as I know that is what he had planned to do. It was the one year anniversary of our initial meeting. But he never made it. I spoke to him for the last time around 9:30 pm and the way he spoke I knew something was not right. He was saying things that did not make since, and he was not himself or nice. After we hung up I laid there trying to fall asleep with tears in my eyes. I was hurting I didn't not understand. I had a very bad feeling. I tried to fully get what was going on but my mind just couldn't comprehend. Ten minutes after lying awake hurting I finally felt peacefulness wash over me and I drifted off to sleep. Around 2:30pm I was awoke by my dogs barking and a knock at the door. My heart jumped as I woke from my slumber not knowing who could be at my door. Hoping it was Rocky yet fearful it was something else. I opened the door to two police men who were looking for the wife or next of kin of Rocky. The first thing I noticed was a drop of blood on his shirt that he did not know was there. I knew right then what I had feared all along. My Rocky was gone. I invited them in I was in complete shock. They explained that he had been in a car accident and wasn't wearing his seat belt. Then they explained to me what I needed to do. When they left. I began to sob. I remembered what he had just began telling me about a month before "Baby girl you are my first love and I know you will be my last love, death before I dishonor my loyal and loving wife" How could he know I thought to myself? I began to scream at Rocky. How could he leave me alone? How could he just throw away our love? I didn't know how

I was going to survive without him. I felt an emptiness sweep through my body. The love of my life was no longer on earth. No more would he walk through our door. No longer would I hear "I love you Baby girl" Never again would he stroke my hair and look into my eyes. I was completely lost all over again. I walked into our room and wrapped up in his jacket that he had left. It still smelt of him, I couldn't imagine never being able to smell that scent again. I looked at my ring that he made me. It had always been big and hard for me to wear but my friend Amy had given me the idea at this time to put it on a chain. I found a necklace with angel wings and added my ring to it. From then on I never took it off and added a dream catcher amongst other things to it later.

Needless to say I didn't go back to sleep. I talked to a couple of friends just because I didn't want to be alone. I called his family to break the bad news. Little did I know that my wifely duties would be stripped from me. I won't go into the details because I don't like to live too much in the past or blame people who weren't thinking clearly. To make a long story short I was pushed away by my in-laws and told some things that made me question if our marriage was real. I thought I had no rights. I know now it had a lot to do with needing someone to blame and to take over the arrangements. This isn't to say anything bad about the family because up until then everything was fine between us and I had really grown to love them. This hurt me and kept me from grieving. I didn't understand why at the time they pushed me away. I know more now. After a stressful and hurtful process just to receive some of my husband's ashes I held a cry ceremony with a couple of my closest friends. It was beautiful; I felt he was there with me somehow. Since he was Native American I made a handout with a special poem:

I am the breeze that kisses your cheek...I am the sun that warms your face...when you look at the purple evening sky, it is me. When you see a majestic mountain it is me...When the birds sweetly sing...it is my voice...when the water gently laps against the shore it is my heartbeat...I am the green grass against your feet. I am the refreshing shade of summer. In the stars you see my eyes... IN the blue sky you see my body. Feel the air that surrounds you, I am there. Feel the love in your heart. I am there... Author unknown...

I put a cross at the site that said "In loving memory of my Husband Rocky" with the dates and R&R love. This cross was placed down the hill a bit and another cross was placed by the freeway. I played music from a CD I had made for him although the CD player that my friend swore she just checked wouldn't play this caused me to pull my car up and use its CD player...Earlier in the yr. he had carved a happy face into the front of the car...so now this happy face of his was right in the middle of the ceremony....was this somehow a sign?... We all laughed saying that Rocky was really there. I then read the beautiful card he had written me with tears in my eyes and streaming down my face; I couldn't help but cry my heart was torn to pieces. I placed some of his ashes in a dot on my forehead; this was a Native tradition to keep the spirit of your husband with you always. I wanted to honor our native ways and in doing so honor him and who he truly was. Rocky had showed me amazing sides to himself that he never shared with anyone. He was a truly beautiful person when he was himself. He was charming and funny, it was only the outside influences that he allowed to take him over as he tried to numb the pain of his past that shadowed how he truly was. I saw all his beauty on the inside and out. He was a part of me and I was a part of him. I was surrounded by friends who loved me yet I felt so alone. I was angry.... a year of knowing him just wasn't long enough. I was lost. I didn't know how I was going to survive, I already felt like a piece of me was missing when we were apart now I would never hold him or feel his lips on mine again. Never would I fall asleep to the beat of his heart as I did every night.

I wrote this shortly after he passed:

"I am thankful that I was blessed to have been given the chance to love someone who needed it more than I did. I felt more love in a little bit of time than I ever had in my whole life despite difficulties and I miss our good times. I miss his voice...hugs, kisses and the way he made me feel about him and myself. Our destiny was tied together for a reason and I know I made him happy and he felt more love than he ever thought he could and that is all that matters."

It was hard for me to stay at home because I saw him every place in the house. So I stayed with my mother for a couple of weeks. I had to make a change so I decided to paint the inside of house so I could start staying there again. It just needed to be different in order for me to be able to even go inside. It was weird being in our house without him. I couldn't escape the loss and loneliness I felt. I would call his cell phone every day about 15 times a day just to hear his voicemail until it was shut off. It was the only way I could get through the day. People tried to be there for me but they didn't understand what I was going through. I was torn apart. I kept seeing the accident in my mind's eye every time I closed my eyes or wasn't busy for a second... it was hard to get the image of what my thoughts pictured may have happened out of my head. Rocky is the love of my life...him and my son made up my world now a piece of that world was missing. My nights filled with tears, I missed sleeping on his chest and listening to his heart. That had been the way we slept every night. I couldn't imagine not feeling his warm body next to mine and him holding me as I slept. My days were filled with wondering how I was going to go through life without him. My soul ached for one more kiss...talk...hug...but I knew that was impossible. My love was gone or was he?

My writings to him" It seems to be getting more difficult as time moves on, reality is finally setting in that you're not coming home. I will never again hear your heartbeat or feel your kisses. Yet I feel you with me everywhere...I see you in my dreams every night and sense you in my heart. I changed the house so it's not so hard but I know you love the way it has turned out. I just need the strength to go back and stay there. I am trying to look at it as being closer to you. Just hard to not see you there but I know in a way you are because your presence still lingers. The more I think about it the more I realize God had his reasons. Still I miss your love and the way it made me feel...I know you love me and you feel my love for you still as strong as ever...there will never be a replacement for you in my heart. You are the love of my life...please continue to watch over us and I will see you again one day...I love you my love and always will"

Chapter 3: Reaching out from Beyond

Shortly after Rocky passed away I began to feel a presence. Like he was there with me in a way. I had this overwhelming feeling that he needed to speak to me. Strange things began to happen. He began coming in my friends dreams who had never even met him. One of those friends named Koly has a daughter who is gifted in certain ways. Koley told me what had happened. Her daughter was talking to someone. Koly asked her who she was talking to? This little girl said this man named Rocky. She described him perfectly said he had long hair and loved stars (Rocky had been a fan of the cowboys) but also he had always told me we were written in the stars. Others began to contact me about dreams they were having. I had always been a spiritual person and believed in such things as spirit and ghosts. But had never really experienced it firsthand. Only just a few experiences in my life that I may bring up later. Little did I know this was just the beginning of many other amazing things that would happen and would prove to me just how love continues beyond death.

One day while sitting at work the door sounded like it creaked opened. When I got up to look no one was there but it was slightly ajar. There was no wind and it had been closed completely. The phone at work would beep like it was off the hook but it wasn't. While driving home from work I was getting ready to cry when all of a sudden there was this goofy looking crane bird in the middle of the road. I started to laugh and say "ha ha funny Rocky" the bird looked at me and flew off. Those kinds of birds were not common in that part of the city. I started to look up things and found out that spirit can use animals to contact us. Was my husband trying to reach out to me from beyond??

One evening my phone rang it was my friend so I answered it. It was dead air so I hung up and called her back. She said she didn't call me but was talking to someone about calling me. Hum that was strange I thought to myself. I would leave my phone on the charger till it was completely charged but it wouldn't stay that way. It would die in the middle of the night which didn't make sense as a charge usually held for a couple of days. I had begun doing more research as these things were happening and found out that spirit can use batteries or electricity to communicate with us. I believed that was what was going on. Me and my friend Koly had been talking about a tattoo I wanted to get and were discussing maybe Baby girl! Just then I received a text from Koly it said "Babygurl I love you ;)" When I asked her about this, she said, "I didn't send that to you I swear...I've even looked in my texts and it is not there" I asked her if she was sure and she said yes she was positive.

I received a beautiful text from a friend that had stayed with me on the phone the night he passed... on May 31, 2012 that I wanted to share with you: "He did love you despite that BS...If you have nothing else Raya you have so much love. You give it freely and I hope you are aware of how much love is pointed back at you too from so many people."

I had appreciated her loving words but I still felt so alone. I had spoken to a friend about certain things I was experiencing and she put me in touch with a lady who hears from spirit. Little did I know this would start a chain of events and messages that would make me realize just how strong our connection was and how much he was around me.

Text on June 23, 2012"I am sorry I just can't do it tonight too beat. It's not fair to you; stuff is starting to come as I think of you. Always start off with small wilt flowers. Perhaps bits of yellow ones too in the dirt. Don't know if it means much now just wanted to share.

June 25, 2012...8:36 am: "Wanted to share...when I was talking to you I noticed the Jenga game box on the stool was rocking back and forth a little bit when we were talking about his hair. I just want over to test it and there was no way it could have moved by itself, it may mean nothing. I am constantly learning new ways of communicating. I am not right all the time but I always share in hopes of validating and getting messages across as well. I am learning to trust myself ...This is really bugging me gonna go for a walk and think about this. What does Red & Rocky mean? Summersaults or rolling?" After this I explained to her that Red was Rocky's favorite color but also the color of the car he was in...Rocky is his name and the summer salts is

21

probably because he was in a car accident. She replied "Ok I feel like you have helped me validate him. He is quite frantic trying to get your attention. This is what I am getting, Getting over the guilt, anger almost shame that he has caused, his anger created a quick death...his issues, his problems, his shame. Do not hold yourself accountable for any part of that accident. Second, he wants to talk about the relationship and why he did the things he did. Third, to remember the amazing love and connection that was and is. You got a lot going on and a long road ahead. Just remember he is going to be with you getting you through it. Make any sense? And the ones that hear him are the true ones that are going to help you with your hearts best interest. People are going to try and take advantage of you right now." I told her she had hit on a lot of the things that had been going through my mind. This made me realize that I was experiencing certain things and that this was going to get very interesting to say the least. A few days later she told me that she vaguely remembered a long hair guy trying to talk to her. He was saying "Help her" but she wish that she remembered more. During all of this I had some scary things going on with his family and I was very frightened. I won't go into it because I don't feel it's important. But she sent me a text saying "Hey how are you today? Crazy thing...I felt compelled to drive by your house around 4am after work last night....I got the since it was super protected and was almost afraid to drive past it. Looks like you are much protected. Will see you soon. Any crazy dreams?" After this I felt a little better. I had been getting dreams at the time but hadn't been writing things down. I didn't learn to do that till later. Next I was going to meet with her and see what Rocky had to say.

Finally it was time for my meeting with the medium. This lady that came to my house knew nothing of our relationship as I told her no information. During the reading Rocky said he was sorry for the things that happened during our relationship. He was going to protect me and he was there at that moment playing with my hair, just as he always did. He told me to go to the beach and put some of his ashes into the water and mourn since I hadn't had a chance to do so with everything that was going on. He talked about him and the person he was with the night of his passing arguing about money and coming home to me. His love for me was overflowing and the medium said she had never seen anything like it before it was so strong. He said that he sees how much I love him now. He had been in trouble doing the wrong things but he did it all for me. He wanted to take me to the beach and it was like everything he did was all for me. He liked the idea of the tattoo but said to put it in a naughty place with a laugh. (Totally something he would say) He said that he loved me so much and he was so sorry for everything. The things I thought that were going on were actually happening and he is sorry for the certain people he hung around and that he wasn't strong enough to fight his issues. He brought up Magic Mountain and the beach as two of the best times of his life that we had together. During this Reading I wish I would've written everything down. But it confirmed all that I had known in my heart. When she left I sat on the couch. She had told me he would stay with me for a bit. I relaxed and closed my eyes. I could feel him holding me as a sense of peace washed over me.

After that day I began to notice things that were happening around me. I asked for a sign and two butterflies flew towards my window and Rocky's name entered my mind at the same time. I punched R into my phone without even thinking. I noticed certain things happening in the house. I was in the shower and I heard this slam... I got out of the shower to notice that the door slammed shut then the light from the fixture fell. I felt like he was definitely trying to get my attention. I noticed that his ashes had been moved as well. I remember hearing something from Sylvia Browne about leaving a tape recorder out. So I decided to do that. I was surprised by what I heard the next day when I listened. At the very beginning of the tape it said WTF I'm sorry. Turns out I had just been cussing him out and yelling at him for leaving me. This was his way of telling me that he was with me and he was sorry. If you knew him like I did you would get it. In the tape you can hear the dogs start to go crazy because of the energy I suppose. I noticed that my phone would be on the charger all day but would be dead. My son and I would see butterflies everywhere. The TV would keep going on and off or messing up. One night I woke up to a shadow over my bed. I freaked out because of what had been going on in my physical life and how I had been threatened I thought someone was in my house. After thinking about it I wondered if that could've been him. On the night of my birthday I had been of course drinking. When I got into bed I was crying and crying and talking to him. On my last birthday I had went to see him because he was in jail for something he did not do but because he was around the person that did he still had to go to court. So I had went to see him and I remember us holding our hands up with the glass in between just trying to touch in a way and feel each other's warmth. So this Birthday I had missed him terribly. All of a sudden I felt this feeling of peace again and like two arms around me. I felt at ease and I knew at that moment he was holding me and I was finally able to fall asleep.

On my birthday I had went to see Sylvia Browne. I didn't get picked for a reading but the lady next to me did. Turns out she was a medium and had asked Sylvia to confirm that she was. Which she did. After she came back to the seat she gave me her number and told me I needed to call her. So I did and when we finally spoke this was her message to me from Rocky. Again she knew nothing about us. "He confirmed that he did hold me the night I was crying and that it was in deed him that had been watching me while I slept. He never meant to scare me. He said that he was sorry and I was right about him wearing his seatbelt. Click it or Ticket. He said he was sorry about his family and how they treated me. They were wrong to do what they did to me. He should've never left me to be with them he just didn't want to lose his family but he was wrong. The fight was so stupid and it should've never happened and he is sooo sorry. That it wasn't him talking the night he passed it was the alcohol and he is sorry. He mentioned the clothes that I and my friend Shannon had just put under the bed. He told me that he does in deed mess with the TV. (Because that was something we did a lot together was watch TV) He told me to get an Indian statue for my son so that he knows Rocky watches over him and can see it. He said "I love you Baby girl."

Some of the things that happened I wasn't keeping track of because I didn't think of it at the time. But once I started realizing it I began keeping track even if it was just little things. I believe now that spirit always brings us to people we are meant to meet. As my journey continued Rocky was bringing me to people who were helping me get through all of this. I had begun to read books to understand how this all worked. It was beginning to help me gain some knowledge in the subject of life after death and the way that spirit communicates with us. Through Facebook I met a Master Clairvoyant named Rachel Mai.

She became my friend and offered me a few readings. I also started taking classes with her. She explained to me that Rocky and I were Twin Flames. This was going to take some digging to find out exactly what this was but little did I know everything would start to make since...our relationship, the trials, the struggles and the reasons why would all start to become clear.

Chapter 4: Twin Flames

So I wanted to explain exactly what Twin Flames are. Now I have become sort of an expert on them since all of this has came to pass. So In the beginning twin flames, one soul, were split into two. Male and female energies. Each carrying a part of the soul. This would be described as Yin and yang which is the symbol for Twin Flames. Light and dark. A balance when united. Which if you remember I used to call Rocky the yin to my yang. So on a soul level I knew exactly what we were to each other. Usually the Twins don't incarnate together. But there have been lives where they have been together. More in a soul mate form. Now from the research I've done there are different takes on this. But I now know lives that I've had with him...So I know that we have had other lives together. We only ever get ONE Twin Flame. We can have many soul mates but only one other true half of our soul. So when Rocky said we were written in the stars...he was right...as in we were always meant to be. Our destiny was tied together. On a soul level we both knew that as well. Twin Flame love is a Divine love not just a normal love. It is felt deep within and when the two unite it is always for a purpose and when the souls are ready. Not many twins make it because the souls are not able to withstand the power of the twin flame union. It's like in a way looking in a mirror. This is when there is a runner and a chaser. The runner is usually the male but can be the female. From what I have seen in the other Twin Flame Unions that I have encountered... the male is the dark half and the female is the light half most of the time. The female is always trying to save the male who usually has a very tough life and has to endure a lot of different things which impact him on a soul level. This is why I've noticed a lot turn to drugs or alcohol to be able to deal with life. Also it's hard for these souls to be here as they are evolved.   I'm sure there are cases when it is reversed but I haven't seen one yet. Dark forces will always try to break up twin flames. As one happy twin flame couple emits as much light as if all of Europe was to attain enlightenment. Many times the dark forces are able to take hold of one of the twins with addictions of some kind. This makes them weak to the darks intentions. Which the dark is always trying to cause much harm to the relationship and to them as humans. Many times they are even taken over by demons and such during their ups of the addiction. Also it doesn't always have to be a male and female. Twin flames can also exist physically in same sex relationships as well as it doesn't always have to be a love relationship either. It just mostly is. With twin flames there is immense passion...and you are drawn to each other in a way that is really too powerful to describe. It's like Magnetism. This is why I was so drawn to Rocky from the moment I met him and was already in love with him.   People always argue if there is love at first site, with twin flames and often soul mates there are. There is always a sense of familiarity, where you just know you have known them before. Feeling as if you have finally found your home or your other half. The feeling is unlike any you have ever experienced before. All of this I experienced with Rocky. When I started learning about all of this it was like finally it all makes since! With Twin flames there are lots of Synchronicities that surround the relationship as well as numerology. The basic Twin Flame numbers are 8 and 11. Later on when I was curious to see if we had any numerology so I added up our Life path numbers. His is 4 and mine is 7. Together that makes 11. The way you find your life path number is your full birth date added until it is a single digit. We were married on 11/4/11...11 being twin flame number and 4 being his life path number. I would always see 11:11 on the clock which is another sign. I still see this number although it is also related to the fact that I am a star seed. There will be more on that later as well. The day we met May, 26, 2011 equals 8. Twin Flames feel like they will die without the other. This is why I couldn't breathe when he would leave and would fight his leaving. No matter how hard the relationship was. With anyone else I most likely would've left but with twin flames it is very hard to be apart. It is just a very intense relationship and connection. As previously stated the dark will always try to break up a Twin flame couple. In our case it seemed as if all odds were against us and we were constantly fighting for our relationship. Dark people and circumstances always tried to tear us apart. Rocky was not strong enough to fight it..He was the runner. Things were beyond his control really. People with addictions are often enticed by demons and dark entities to do bad things and behave in a way that is not normal for them. I know now that is what was happening with Rocky...he would get taken over. The dark may have won the physical war. But without all of this happening I would not have found my true calling or be helping as many people has we have. Twin Flames rarely meet as

27

twin flames...but more are now coming together because of the changes that are going on. They are reuniting to help with the transitions and shifts. They say that once you have met your Twin and are with them as a Twin that it is your last life... Twins can become your guides once they pass. Most of the time our loved ones can't become our guides if they have had a recent life with you and pass, although I have heard it happens but rarely. But they must be a very advanced soul. However our twins can always become our guides. I know that Rocky is my guide and he guides me still every day, he is who I listen to and first began hearing. I think that is why he has become my main guide because I have been able to hear him the easiest because of the connection that we have always had. In the chapters that follow you will get even a better understanding of how our love has continued and that even though he is on the other side...he is able to help me and love me so much better than he ever could when he was here. So the dark did not win because together we are making great strides.

People that have an idea of what Twin Flames are but have never met them always tend to want to find their other half. All relationships mirror the Twin Flame union. I know I found mine when I least expected and when I was not looking. Matter of fact I had just said I was giving up on love when he crossed my path in a way I never expected. Honestly though Twin Flame unions although intense and full of passion is not easy. As I stated before many do not make it just because the dark does succeed and one half will have a ton of struggles they cannot overcome. There can be a lot of trying times, ups and downs as the dark tries to come in-between you. Also if the souls are not ready it can make the relationship hard and not work out. Some examples of famous Twin Flames are Romeo and Juliet, and Guinevere and Lancelot. It seems to be a forbidden love most of the time with always a great fight to endure to be together. Many may not understand why you put up with so much to be with the other or why you fight so hard. The truth is your soul cannot help it. It longs to become one and when united in many ways it is amazing, but you are never the same. So it's not all peaches and cream as many would think. Not in a physical reality anyway. Now when your Twin is on the other side things are different. There is a new perspective that opens up, along with the twin on the other side wanting to help you along your path. They do this before they incarnate as well. You each help each other in your lives that you are not physically in together, and when you are on the other side together it is bliss. It's mostly the human aspects along with trials, and the dark that make it so hard for Twin Flames to survive.

When you're separate from your Twin Flame doesn't matter if it's when you are both alive or not. You can experience astral meetings. Including astral sex. Yes this does exist. You have this bond and even when you are apart your astral bodies can still experience things. You can feel what the other is feeling even if you are not on the same room. You can share images and visions as well. It is really a psychic connection unlike any other.

Chapter 5- Addiction

After sort of explaining a bit about Twin flames I wanted to talk about some things I left out in the previous chapters and explaining them from a spiritual standpoint. I struggled a lot with writing this chapter but was given guidance and permission. In hopes to help others with addiction or those who have loved ones that struggle from addictions understand things from a different perspective.

What you have to understand here is that the moment Rocky met me he was immediately violently psychically attacked by the darker forces. It caused him to go sort of crazy in a way. This would happen to anyone that was attacked in the way he was. I learned later that Rocky Struggled with addictions. Both drugs and alcohol. This was his way of coping with not only his past but the attacks. When he was in a high or drunk state I did not recognize who he was. Rocky was not there. Instead it was a monster that sort of emerged. I watched addictions tear this beautiful person down and change him into something he wasn't. When Rocky was sober he was the most amazing loving man I have ever met. During those times we were extremely happy... but when he was under the influence of something Rocky was no longer present. I now understand from a spiritual view this was in order to break us apart because of the light we illuminated. In the paragraphs that follow I am going to talk about some of the things that happened. In hopes not to talk bad about Rocky but so that people can maybe relate and I can bring awareness of the things that addictions can cause people to do. Also, I know that Rocky would want to share the story in order to help others, as it is part of our path together. After all Twin flames always have a higher spiritual purpose.

Some of the time that Rocky was in prison he began exhibiting behaviors that weren't normal. However being so in love with him I overlooked a lot, thinking that he suffered from a mental illness due to all his time in prison and the bad things that had happened in his life. I found out later that was some of it as I do feel he had some mental disorder but also I was told by his family at one time he had been diagnosed while in prison but I don't know how true this is, however it does make since and I feel like the path he choose with addictions made the disorder worse. He would always think I was going to leave him. He began thinking that I wasn't coming to see him alone. That I was bringing others with me which was not true. I would argue with him about this a lot. One time I was picking up a rental car and he thought I had a guy with me and that is why I was late but of course that was not the case. There was a few times when I was visiting him that he swore I was looking at other inmates. This was not true as I only had eyes for him and this was so far out of my element I would never do that. He even got upset walked out and he refused to see me. Of course the CO's took this opportunity to ask me why I was even with him. He had these insecurities and we would argue intensely about them I was always on the defense. Also I remember one conversation he thought I was some type of spy. That was kind of out there. I feel that to this day he was able to get high in prison. Although when I would talk to him and the subject of drugs would come up he would say he couldn't even take aspirin. That he didn't do drugs and never had. Of course you're probably saying to yourself right now. Well that's a lot of red flags. Yes it was. But what you have to understand is that Twin flame love is extremely powerful. All you can do is think the best of your other half and all you want to do is be there for them regardless of how they act. Ever heard the expression blinded by love. Well that was me. He would go back to his normal loving self and I would just melt. It was beyond my control. We truly loved each other and no matter what follows in the paragraphs, I need you to know that love never faded. I always saw the best in him and he was always an amazing person it was just he was not in control anymore, he was spiraling, the drugs and alcohol had taken his beauty away, and turned him into someone he was not. He was definitely being used by dark forces. I also want to stress here that my son was never involved in this. He was never at home when this would take place as he liked to spend time with his grandmother or was at his dad's. Rocky was always good to him no matter what he treated him as his own son. So to this day that is how my son sees him, as someone who was there for him and did all the things with him a father should. So what went on between me and Rocky was between us. Eli never saw it or experienced it. I think he had seen Rocky tipsy at times but it was never to this crazy stage that I will go into. Rocky was away a lot or out of the house a lot. My son was

31

never in danger, I would always put him first. What you have to understand is that with twin flames the attraction is so powerful and the one half always wants to save the other half. So they will endure hell if they have to. I am not condoning what he did; abuse or giving excuses, and until someone walks in another's path there should never be judgment. I knew the Rocky I loved was in there somewhere and he was fighting hard, that came to light in the times he was beautiful and in how he treated my son. I did learn later that Rocky had an attachment it had attacked me after he passed and followed me to my new home. He was also in all the pictures of me and Rocky, I noticed this after my gifts came to light. I am now attachment free...but I need to stress here that dark attachments can make a person think and act in a way they normally wouldn't. In sort of a possession way. They can cause a person to drink, do drugs, be angry, think negatively, and all around change a person for the worse.

When he got out of prison and we were living together things were good for a little while. He did drink one time and went back to jail overnight. This was my first look at his alcoholism. He had gotten violent and went inside of a bar and said all kinds of crazy things. I was not home at the time but was at work. I only heard what he had told me. This is going to be hard for me to remember how everything went because there was so much. But in the paragraphs to follow I will talk about the events I can remember the most.

I would come home from work in the beginning and he would have the house cleaned and things done. So that I would not have to worry about it. But the times he would go away to see his parole officer; where there were bad influences he would come back different. One night I remember He was sleeping with a knife. He swore that there were people outside or something. He was extremely paranoid. This made me think that maybe it was because he had to watch his back so much in prison. It seemed go back and forth from being normal to being kind of well strange. As it got worse and he got deeper in things started to become well even weirder. He would call me at work and say things like I was cheating on him and during our conversation although there was no one in the office he would say there was. He would check my clothes when I came home for any type of stains. I would always tell him "I only want you I'm not a cheater. I would never cheat on you. I only want to be with you forever." He always thought he would see stains that weren't there.

I feel like I have blocked a lot out. But one time he was drunk and I was home. He had started saying a bunch of stuff about other men. The same stuff he always seemed to say when he was drunk. Started telling me stuff about his life and bad things he had done. Which I do not know if any of it is true, or if he was just trying to scare me. He was not himself and would not listen to reason. This was the first time he ever laid hands on me. He pulled my hair and threw me around a bit. Then he left. I'm thinking the timeline may be a bit off on some of these events.

He would be so normal and loving sometimes and other times it was like he continued to be controlled by the dark. Another time I vaguely recall is once again he was saying that I had cheated on him and that I wasn't honest with him. I just needed to be honest with him. He had been drinking. I hated when he drank he was not the man I loved when he had any kind of alcohol. This time things seemed to escalate. He started breaking pictures in the house. He would even threaten to throw down my big lizard tank. He would grab my hair and throw me around. I would get up and fight back. But I was not strong enough. When I was thrown against a half broken window in my room my head hit the glass and broke the rest of it. During this time I would cry and scream and tell him that I was faithful to him. I didn't know why he did these things. My arms would be held back to where I thought my shoulders were going to break. He would put me in a choke hold. He would hit me in places where there would leave no marks. I remember him taking me by my hair and just dragging me or bringing me up to where he could throw me across the room. I would just be severely sore afterwards and to emotionally broken. So that the next day I would call into work sick. After he had come down from being drunk he would start saying I didn't mean to do any of that. I don't know why I did it. I don't remember things; you know that's not me. He would hold me and say he was sorry and it would never happen again. It was as if something had intruded his body and done these things then left. His eyes were soulless during these times. Almost like a possession or oppression, which is the time before a possession. Honestly I felt like I was in a nightmare I couldn't wake up

33

from. I loved him so much for the man that I knew he truly was but during those times I could not see this man. I lived day to day not knowing what was to happen next also constantly defending myself.

One day I got home and he had gone through my personal things where I kept all of my memories. Some were old letters. He asked me why I had them. I said I just hadn't gone through everything and I was keeping them for old memories. The ones from my son's dad were going to be for him some day. After arguing for what seemed like hours, he made me get rid of all of those letters and old things.

Another time we went to his uncle's to hang out. We thought it would be a nice time to introduce me to him. He was very nice man. Actually after Rocky passed he was the only one that spoke to me and tried to help me. Anyway, there was alcohol there. I begged Rocky not to drink but he did anyway promising he wouldn't get out of hand. Which never happened he always got out of hand just the way alcohol affected him. He started thinking I was into another guy that was there or that I was looking at his uncle a certain way. It was all very strange behavior once again. I remember we were going on a walk or something and he started in. He started to pull my hair. So I took off and went into a field and cried. This was all at night in the pitch black. He began looking for me frantically. Finally when I thought it was ok I came out. I vaguely remember being in front of a house and an argument happening and him starting to be abusive and then sheriff pulling up. We said we were just going for a walk. During this time his uncle was a bit worried but didn't know what was going on. After we went back in the house the arguing about these little things happened most of the night. Until the next morning and he was fine as always. He had to get up early for a class that his uncle was sending him to so he could work with him. He went to class but was a bit weird with me because his uncle and I had been alone in the car. Before we left we went to lunch and he was weird again. Saying things that didn't make sense. His uncle knew something was up and asked if I was ok. I sort of explained what Rocky was saying. I believe that his Uncle had a talk with him about it.

I remember on Thanksgiving he was up all night checking my phone and I guess going on my Facebook. I had old messages in there from

34

old friends that I knew almost all of my life. Yes some were guys but I had not spoken to them recently or even after Rocky and I had begun talking. A few were ex's or old flames but we had just remained friends. When you live in a small town you know a lot of people. I had stopped all communication with any other guys after Rocky and I got together. I had sort of quit talking to everyone and became isolated, in order to make him happy and believe that I was faithful to him. More faithful than I had ever been to anyone. He was saying there were conversations that weren't even in the thread, and that I was still talking to these guys when there were no messages to even back it up. It was like all in his imagination. He wanted me to tell him about all the guys in high school that I had a crush on or went out with and would go through my friends wanting to know how I knew them. I went through these accusations all night. On the way to his family's house the conversation continued. Then when we arrived for dinner he just decided to be over it. When I would go out in public to the store with him especially that time I had to keep my eyes down because he would think I was looking at guys. It was hard for me because I'm a people watcher. That was something he thought was an excuse. I felt like I was constantly trying to prove to him how much I loved him and that there was no one else. Many times during this he said he was going to leave me and I would get so depressed and he would feel bad and stay. It was a game that was being played. Push and pull. Runner and chaser.

On Christmas Eve they had these puppies outside of the Market. Eli begged and begged me for one and I had been thinking we needed a big dog anyway. She was so sweet and beautiful. We instantly fell in love and I caved. We took her home and Rocky started saying that some guy had given her to me for Christmas. Elijah and I both said "no we got her from in front of the market" He didn't believe us of course.

I recall I was super excited for our first Christmas together. He seemed to be too. We went shopping for Elijah and wrapped the presents. On Christmas Eve my mom was up and he was acting very weird. He began looking out the window constantly and just acting super paranoid. He began arguing with me that I was looking at someone outside. Nothing he said was making any sense. My mom stayed with Eli in his room while I argued with him in the bedroom. Basically defending myself again. Needless to say he ended up leaving me on Christmas Eve and went down to his cousin's house. Eli went to his dad's the next day and so I ended up just being alone. I would cry and cry. I felt so broken. I didn't understand what was going on. He would call me and we would talk...sometimes he was normal sometimes not. I begged him to come home. Finally after 3 days he asked me to pick him up. So I went down to get him. His wedding ring I had gotten him for Christmas was gone. He said he threw it out of the window. After all of this I still took him back and wanted him to be with me.

New Year's we had a pretty good new year's day. Then we went to his family's house. Everything started out really good. We had a nice new year's kiss but he had continued to drink. For some reason we were talking to his aunt about us. We told her that we had gotten married. Then he started in about stuff and I can't even remember to this day what it was about. I just remembered that he broke his phone and was sort of saying all kinds of hurtful things. Needless to say as the alcohol wore off we decided to go home and he was very sick on the way back to the house. The next day he was fine and we kind of just relaxed all day. It seemed though that this was a turning point thought. Because the following year would be worse then I could've ever imagined.

We would always celebrate our Anniversary on the 4th and 6th of every month. With some sort of card or letter. To celebrate on the 4th of January he had written me a letter apologizing for things and saying they were going to be different. Of course when I came home he had been drinking. But also at this time I feel like other substances were involved. When I got home from work I was greeted with his letter and gave him mine. Well mine wasn't good enough. Something in it set him off. Majorly. Again I did not recognize him all of a sudden. He flew into a rage, It was as if Rocky was temporarily gone and something else had taken control. We began arguing I don't even remember over what other then he would start in about how I was cheating on him at work. About things that didn't even make sense. Then the abuse began, this time I was held up in the room and he would hit me in the ribs, face or stomach. Without leaving bruises. He

36

even put his arm around my neck and made me pass out. I remember coming to and he was sitting on the end of the bed. Just looking at me. Through eyes that were cold and dark honestly he looked like a demon. The man I loved was not him anymore. The monster had taken over. The argument started again. He would throw me around and hold my arms back and it felt like my shoulders were going to break, bend my wrists back. I would get away but of course he was stronger than me. He would grab me by my hair and drag me. Then throw me around some more. He kept saying he was going to slash my tires on the car because I kept saying I was going to leave. I just wanted my loving Rocky back, where had he gone? He began packing a bag like he was going to leave, tore up our marriage certificate and some of the letters that I had from him. He acted like he was going to throw over the lizard tank again. I would unpack his bag even though at this point I was scared of him.... I need to remind you that twin flames feel like they will die without the other although he was putting me through hell I didn't want him to leave. It's very hard to explain, and I'm sure even harder to understand if you have not experienced this sort of intense love. I remember at one point running across the street to get away from him because he was so out of control. Throwing things and hurting me. I remember going back in the house later when I felt it was safe. Honestly I can't remember how it ended if he left or what. I remember that he calmed down all of a sudden and the rage stopped. Like Rocky had returned back into his body. I think that I ended up going back into my room and just sleeping there. Keeping my distance from him. The next morning I called in for work as I was too sore and too emotionally broken to even consider going to work. Plus I did not want my coworkers to suspect anything. Again he would say how he was sorry he didn't know what happened or why he acted this way. He could not even recall the events. He was just as confused as I was but yet he still was not strong enough to fight back against the addictions or the dark forces behind them.

Toward the end of the month of January, I guess you could say that I was being looked after by a higher power. He had gotten in trouble at his cousins while drinking. I will not go fully into the details here but because it was a violation of his parole this landed him back in jail. In a way I was happy because I felt in Jail maybe he could sober up, since he was fighting for his life as this case would be a third strike. However I had witnessed the whole thing and in the situation he did nothing wrong other then he shouldn't have been there. I was praying that he would come out differently since his life was on the line if he got out depending on how the case went. I know that was a scary time for him. I stood by him and helped him out with the case as much as I could. Even tried looking for a good lawyer. He was in for a little over a month. Eli and I went to see him for my birthday and I remember putting my hand on the glass to touch his, kind of like what you see in movies. I remember him being the Rocky I knew and fell in love with. I would keep money on my phone so that we could talk often. He kept apologizing for everything he had done wrong and promised that things would be different when he got out. This was when he started saying "Death before I dishonor my loyal and loving wife." Since he wasn't around for my birthday or Valentine's Day he sent me a card with a wedding ring that he made out of string, it had R&R luv embroidered on it. This was the ring that never fit me right. Below is what the card said, and this is how he truly was when he was sober.

My most loving, loyal and beautiful wife. Your more to me than any one person has ever been. You're my friend, my lover, my dog and best of all my wife, and without a doubt, I say this with my utmost sincerity, you're so much better than my dream girl and you're my whole life! I swear you're a special woman, truly an amazing wife. I'm grateful to have even met you and you can't fathom the amount of honor I feel for you giving me your life, love and loyalty. There has been a few times when you love has touched me so deeply I shed a tear and think…"F*** there is no way I deserve this beautiful & amazing woman" Yet I promise and swear with the most sacred vow no one will ever love you as good as I can. You're so special to me. I adore you and love you with every fiber of my being and from the depths of my soul I'll try my whole life to make you feel and believe my words are true! I just wanted to tell you how I feel & care so much about you.

"Let there be no doubt it's you I always dream about, your love, your laugh, your smiling face, hold me like a warm embrace."

Happy Valentine's Day

From the depths of my soul Baby Girl I'm so deeply in love with you. Happy Birthday Baby girl! Happy Valentines. =) Will you be my Valentine Baby Girl? You're my First love and I know you're my Last love. I could never love another the way I love you. I'd rather die before I dishonor you. Truly & beyond eternity I'm only yours! Your Indian & Daddy, MWAH! SHMILY =) R&R Love Beast on the Battlefield
PS. You should've got two roses and a ring in this letter. Let me now ok? SHMILY

As you can see when he was himself and sober he was the most amazing man. The drugs and alcohol along with the dark changed him into someone he was not. I know I keep saying this but I truly want to stress it. Notice how he said I was his first and he knew I would be his last? Intuitively he knew that there was no one else he loved the way he loved me and there never would be. You may be thinking "if he loved you so much why did he abuse you?" Well I honestly believe from watching him and seeing him go through all of it..that he was not in control anymore. The dark had marked us and it would continue to try and tear us apart.

After he got out he was doing really well for a while. He actually was amazing. There was no drinking or seemed to be any drugs. He promised me that he would no longer hang out with his cousin who was a bad influence. He did really well throughout April until about the very end of the month into May. Things took a drastic turn. His cousin needed help with something. I begged him not to go but he did anyway saying it was his family and that was how it all went south again. He would take my car and leave to go with him and not come home till really late. I knew he was falling into his old habits. But he continued to say he wasn't. He would go different places and stay gone for a while then return not being himself. He would start checking my clothes again which you know he always found something that wasn't there. He began saying there were people in the mountains and had me hiking looking for these people that he said were hiding up there. I went with him on a hike to prove to him that there was no one there! He started spending a lot of time in the attic. Sometimes he would stay up there all night. He wouldn't even sleep in the same bed with me most of the time but would be out in the living room instead not sleeping. One time he said he was leaving again packed a bag and left. I cried and cried at that time I didn't understand why he was always leaving. I talked him into coming back and he did but then he was in the attic yet again. I could hear him moving around up there while I was trying to sleep. Things started to kind of spiral even more. He would say that I had people hiding in the attic and when he would go to the bathroom they were coming down and having sex with me. He was always convinced that people were either outside or in the attic. SO once again I was in constant defense of myself. Not understanding what he was talking about half the time. It was an awful way to live. This was a very crazy time. Even crazier than before. By this time my job was suffering as I was missing a lot of work. He would call constantly or we had to be talking all the time. Part of this was because yes it was hard to be away from him and part of it was he was just bored I think a lot of the time. I honestly think that he got into this so much also because he had nothing to really do. Ever heard the saying "Idol hands are the devils work shop?" He hadn't been able to get a job with his background so far. But I also guess that he had opportunities with his uncle that he had turned down. That was when his uncle knew something was wrong. I found out later from his uncle that Rocky did have a history of drug use and said that he knew he was using again. I just wish he would've been forthcoming with that information sooner. I had reached out to his family many times but they continued to say he didn't have a problem, but they weren't living in the hell that I was.

Now this next part I want to talk about was one of the worst times ever. He had already begun to spiral even worse than before. He had begun hanging out with the wrong people even more. I am not really sure how it started to be honest. I just remember he began being very paranoid. So paranoid that he thought the sheriff was watching his house and coming to get him. This is when I was sort of held hostage so that I wouldn't go and tell the sheriff anything. I was basically confined to the corner of the room and my hands were tied behind my back. He kept saying he couldn't go back to jail. He was walking around with a knife worried that they were going to come in after him. I remember looking at him and wondering who he was. He was no

40

longer the man I knew and loved. Whatever it was had taken control over him. He wouldn't admit to needing help so how was I supposed to help him. I had tried to enlist his family for help and they denied he even had a problem. I felt lost. I didn't know what was going to happen at this point. He untied me but made me stay in the corner I was not allowed to leave the room. I remember I was crying hysterically just begging him. He would come in and pull my hair or punch me some place. I remember somehow I got out of the room or he let me out. Like I said I believe I had blocked some of what happened this time out but remember bits and pieces. I remember he had a knife and I was lying on the floor. He was over me and the blade was inches away from my face...I was begging him to not do this. I was telling him that this was not him. His eyes were cold and dark as if he wasn't even in there. It was as if I was looking at a demon again. It was not rocky. It was something far worse. But the Rocky in him somewhere fought back and let me up. It was like I could see the struggle of good vs. evil within. Then it was Almost as if he snapped out of it for just a moment because some more abuse went on after he let me up. I was being thrown about. This time I was tired and I just couldn't fight back any more. Then all of a sudden it ended. I don't exactly remember how. I just know that was a very scary moment. Again later on it was as if he did not know or understand what he had done. This was the last turning point I guess u could say. He would continue to spiral and tell me he was tired of all the lies and was going to leave me. Then he would be normal again for a few days. I talked vaguely about this part in previous chapters but wanted to go into more depth here, this was when he told me that he had to meet his parole officer, and asked me to take him down there. This was when I felt something was off. He was not himself. He kept looking at me and touching my hair. Telling me how much he loved me. Then he would say "why can't you just be honest with me?" It was all very confusing and back and forth and really looking back on it, none of it made any sense. I dropped him off feeling as if it was the last time I would ever talk to him again. This time felt different than it ever had before. When I kissed him I couldn't help feeling it was the last time that our lips would ever touch, or he would ever hold me in his arms. It felt like a goodbye. I had this extreme sadness sweep over me... That was why I followed him once he got out of the car. I needed to know where he was going. When I got home he called me

41

and told me to look in his jacket. There was a letter that I didn't understand. Telling me he was leaving me and all of these bogus reasons why. I just broke down and cried. I had done nothing wrong. I loved him so much and here he was giving up on us for reasons that didn't even exist. I guess you could say that I loved the Rocky I knew was inside. I was able to see past all of his darkness. I loved the Rocky that was the most beautiful man I had ever met. The man that had showed extreme love and made me feels things that I had never felt before. I wanted so bad to save that Rocky, that is why I believe I continued to fight for us, I had no choice, as you never do with Twin Flames. The attraction and love is so immense that they are your addiction. His jacket was the last I had of him. I threw that letter away as I knew it was not him, it sounded nothing like him. As I had wrote in the earlier context. He was not himself the week he was gone. He would call me and be his old loving self-saying he wanted to work things out saying he loved me. Then the next day he would say hurtful things that he wanted a divorce and such. This was not the Rocky I knew. As you can see addictions can cause a lot of pain to both people. After every time something would happen he would not remember and would promise it would never happen again. But the bad influences and addictions began to control his life and his soul. I used to think that if he really loved me enough that he would've stopped for me or gotten help. Truth is everyone is different and drugs take a different hold on those that use. Depending on their own chemistry or how strong the dark force is behind the abuse. They had a strong hold on him and I don't think at this point anything could've saved him because he didn't in truthfulness want to save himself. When people carry addictions they turn into this being that has no control over their actions or life. Most people say well why don't they just stop? It's not that easy for some. Sometimes they are just too far gone. To the point of no return. The dark forces were able to keep him going back to the same people, drugs and alcohol. I have learned that dark forces can do many things in our life and we are not in control when they have taken over. I would've had to understand all of what I do now in order to help him on a spiritual level. Which may in turn helped him with the rest of it. I do believe that the devil in a way was doing his best to keep us apart and to break us down. For our light was just too bright. In a physical since he succeeded. In a spiritual since I believe that we are stronger with Rocky in spirit. He can guide me as much as he wants to from where he is and help me more without all of the other influences. On the other side his love is pure and immense. It had always been there he was just not strong enough as a human to fight against the darkness. I used to not understand addiction but now I do in a whole nother light. People with addictions are no longer in control of their actions they are controlled by the high and the forces that make them want to stay high or drunk. Addictions can cause Psychotic actions and breaks in some people as well. My intent on writing this chapter was not to talk bad about Rocky or our relationship in any way. We had many many loving times together as those are well which are the times I know that he was himself and are the moments I will always cherish forever. Those are the moments I try to focus on because those are the times where I saw the true amazing beautiful soul that Rocky was and wanted to be even if it was just a glimpse here and there. The night he passed I had a plan in effect I was going to call his parole officer to see if he could help me get him help. I was never able to do that, and I was afraid to do it prior. I have come to realize though all of this that Rocky decided to leave his body that night that he passed. He was coming up to our house with his cousin and they had been drinking and who knows what else. He was not himself on the phone; he didn't even make any since. No telling what they would've done to me had he had made it home. He was I believe not in control at this point whatsoever. The intention of the dark side was to snuff out my light or to wreak more havoc on our relationship to bring it to the point of no return. But Rocky's higher self or his soul decided that he had enough of the pain, enough of the abuse and enough of the way he was. In doing so he most likely saved my life. So for that I am thankful. I am thankful that on a soul level he loved me enough to sacrifice himself for me. I wanted to put this excerpt into this book in order to show how addiction can affect people and how the dark forces have a lot to do with addiction. Because of all that I went through I understand it from a different perspective. I can't work now because my body got worse and worse after he passed. I was diagnosed with fibromyalgia and have a lot of back and neck problems most likely from the abuse. I was never forthcoming with the doctors about what I had been through. I never wanted Rocky's problems to be put out there or for there to be blame or judgment. I also didn't want people to think that my son was ever any part of it. Rocky was very private about his life but now he is not driven by ego so it is ok that I talk about these things. I would've never done so if there wasn't a higher purpose behind it. He is now all about helping those who have the addictions but also the loved ones that watch those they love go through it. I carry a lot of emotions about that time in my life and have a lot of flashbacks to the most intense moments and any time that I see someone in the same kind of situation or I see something on TV I am immediately taken back to that time and place. I do not blame Rocky for it. I have come to terms with the fact that he was not himself and that in a way things were out of his control completely. I do realize this was the path that he chose to walk but also as Twin flames we were under constant attack. That is part of being a Twin Flame. He has come through in many readings since then apologizing and to me personally. I see him in a beautiful light healed and whole. He had to go through a life review and people that experience the things that he did in his life have a very hard life review where they have to feel every feeling they made someone else feel that they wronged. So he had to feel all the pain that he caused me or any others. He has learned from it all and so have I. The only things and people I place blame on are the dark forces and the people that would not let him be happy. Every time that he was happy with me they would come in and ruin it. However, I do understand that the dark forces were a part of this as well using others for their will to damage us which sadly in the physical realm they succeeded. Our love continues in its more purest form.

I want to mention in this chapter, there was a time when I swear I was pregnant and had a miscarriage. I had been throwing up and then after this went on for a while. I decided to get a pregnancy test. I never showed up positive, but as most women understand we know our bodies. Then came a time later on where I was bleeding so much I just knew it was a miscarriage. Rocky had always said he wanted a family with me. It was one of his dreams when we would talk and he was himself. Shortly after he passed I found out through a reading that I was pregnant with a son. Sometimes the hormones aren't strong enough to show up. HIs name is Dove. Which has a very powerful meaning of peace. During all the emotional turmoil and abuse I guess I lost him in a miscarriage. He has come to me in my meditations so I know that he does exist. The medium that brought

44

him up in a reading knew things she couldn't possibly know and she's not the only medium who has picked up on him. He is a beautiful boy and although I would love to have a piece of Rocky here with me. I know that in a way he is with his dad looking out for me. HIs family told me it was impossible for Rocky to have children as he had gotten snipped. However Rocky has said in the reading that they didn't know what they were talking about. Since I have met my son on the other side many times when I go on a journey, which I will most likely go into later. I know that he exists!

Shortly after his passing when I had gotten into more of the spiritual world. I found out that I am a star seed; well the awakening of a star seed is often very brutal. The star seeds wakeup call can be drastic, sudden, and harsh, for others it is a process which gently unfolds over years. Even after the awakening the conditions for star seeds varies greatly. Some awaken to a huge understanding of their origin, past life memories, skills, abilities, and purpose for being here on the planet all at once. So in a way I have learned that Rocky and I were meant to go through all of this. It was part of my journey as a star seed. It caused me to wake up and be who I am today. It opened me up to a whole nother world that exists and through the awakening I have grown into my gifts and power. I always feel that we go through things in order to grow and learn from them, or so that we may be able to help others in the same situation. I have found that has been true for me. Without going through every aspect of my life. I would not have been opened to my gifts and the possibilities that await me. I would not have been able to help all of the souls and people that I have helped so far. So in a way I have to be thankful. I feel we should always be grateful for any experience as everything happens for a reason and out of it we can emerge stronger and wiser. After Rocky's passing I was in a shell for a bit, in the darkest part of my soul but a about a year later I broke out of that shell and rose from the ashes, myself and my life transformed.... and as I continue to grow and transform I remember where I was before and where I am now. It is like I have literally shed my skin. Although going through everything I have been through has not been easy but downright painful.....there were times when I literally felt my heart breaking and I found myself asking God "why?" I have to say that it has made me who I am today, stronger, wiser and all around better! I realize that loss and hurt can take us to places where we have never been before. It's when we learn to face our grief and our adversity. We refuse to let it bring us down so that our inner transformation can begin. We endure these things in our life because we are meant to it is part of our lessons and our path. If we let it... grief, hurt, and pain...can give us compassion and the ultimate strength. It can mold us into better human beings and evolve our souls to a higher place. It can awaken and open us up to new possibilities if we allow it to. I know looking back I would've never thought that I would be where I am today although I still struggle I have amazing gifts! Sometimes I have to pinch myself when I work with spirit to realize that this has become my life. With tragedy something in us breaks and opens giving us the ability to grow from something that broke us and ruptured our heart. The journey is not an easy one there are twists, turns, hills and drops but when the ride comes to a stop the feeling that YOU made it in one piece and survived overtakes us. Like the Phoenix we can shed who we have been and become something more, someone of the light who understands what it means to be at that place in turn allowing us to build others up and give them strength to rise up as we have. Sometimes the ultimate sacrifices change us into who we were meant to become. We are never done growing, learning and transforming so our journey doesn't end with rising from the ashes, it continues with the flight through life. So take a look back and see the difference in you from then and now, .know that we are all Phoenix's rising up from the ashes evolving into something bigger and brighter!

At this point I want to share with you something I channeled for my grief group on why we struggle.

You are here to evolve your soul. You've chosen to experience life in order to perfect more rapidly. Start looking at life as something you must survive; it's something that can be fun but also very tedious. The best way to look at life is as a school where bad food is served and the teachers aren't always of the highest caliber. You'll make it through much better if u starts to maintain a sense of humor, self-acceptance and self-knowledge to indicate that you're on track. You alone are responsible for your destiny. Your life was fully planned by you prior to coming back to earth. All of life's joys and sorrows were known beforehand, this is your chosen way to reach perfection. You can change your life only when the soul knows that it's time to move to a different direction or switch gears. Ultimately you will experience everything you planned however painful it may be for the evolvement of soul. You never change your main path you may take detours and little off shoots but the main highway always runs a direct course. There may be sightseeing trips off to the side but you will always return to the main road. You view every single Avenue and nuance of your path before u incarnate...You see all the shortcuts and detours...and if u start veering off too far you start getting depressed. This is the soul's way of reminding u that you are off track. Each life is firmly set into place regardless of how many directions it can take. But you still have a basic road which u travel. Every single thing you experience is planned. That is why there is so much counseling before u incarnate. You not only scan your own life but also other major influences. You are allowed to travel many different roads but must achieve your final goal. Happiness means you elevate your soul, you have everything u need, you're functioning and you're living and working for the higher power. By venting your emotions you can better handle the rough stuff in life. There is nothing wrong with complaining but just make sure it's not something you do all the time. Always stay positive and positive things will come to you. You chose to be challenged more in this life so that you could learn more and your soul would evolve. Hang in there and realize you are learning and gaining more strength than you know. Earth is the heaviest and hardest of all planets by choosing to come here we decided that we needed to go through some crap just so that we can become more spiritually evolved.

Stumbled across the perfect quote to end this chapter:
"Until we have seen someone's darkness, we don't really know who they are. Until we have forgiven someone's darkness we don't really know what love is."
Marianne Williamson

In the chapters that follow I want to focus on the beautiful things. I am going to share with you channeled messages, messages from Rocky through mediums, Meditations, things that happened, signs and visitations along with any poems I may have wrote. The rest of the book is going to prove beyond a reasonable doubt that Rocky is very much alive, healed and whole. My hope is that you will open your mind to a whole new thought process and world. Enjoy

Things started happening after Rocky passed but I at the time did not think to write it down or keep track. Some I have already shared with you in the prior chapters, in the next chapters I will share with you what I remember and when I began to start writing things down. Most will have a date but some may not. Rocky was the first spirit that I began hearing. I used to think I was going crazy. When I would read what I wrote back I realized there is no way that was me. I didn't even remember writing it. So I have come to a place where I can hear him very clearly. I can't seem to find the notebook with all of the beginning channelings but I know now it was extremely real. I was not losing it. I still received many readings as sort of validations of my channelings and because I was still learning I needed to hear from someone else what he was trying to say to me. None of the people that gave me readings knew anything other than a picture. Spirit can move things, manipulate energy such as TV's, lights, fire alarms, etc...send you songs, pop memories or thoughts or others thoughts and then they will say it, send you coins or feathers, send signs in nature such as animals or birds , cause you to feel tingles or chills. Send people into your life that reminds you of them. Just about anything you can think of they can do. Including materialize into shadowy or white figures. Meditations are very real; we can travel to the other side through our thoughts and astral project ourselves there. So in the meditations or journeys I could've not made any of that up myself. If that's maybe what you are thinking? Wait until you read everything and then make that decision.

February 2012
I was missing him very bad on my birthday. I had gone and had a few

drinks. Came home and started crying badly. I missed the good times so much and birthdays always took me back to the time I visited him in jail. So I was crying. And talking to him. All of a sudden I felt this peace come over me and as If I was being held. I could feel this immense love and just comfort. I was able to drift off to sleep

2012

Sometime after he passed I was awakened by a shadow looking over me in bed. The dogs had been barking and a lot had been going on in my life. So I had thought it was an Intruder. I rolled out of bed and began crawling I was completely awake when I saw this. I found out later it was Rocky and he did not mean to scare me he was just watching me as I slept.

I decided to leave a tape recorder out after listening to something on Sylvia Browne about catching EVPS at night. So I left this tape recorder one. When Played back not long after I had hit the record button u hear a voice that sounds like Rocky say "WTF I'm Sorry." Then the dogs began barking as if they heard him. I had just been cussing him out for leaving me sometime before I had turned on the tape recorder. This was his reply in a playful way knowing how he is but also his way of trying to yell back. I got lots of other things on the tape recorder during this time as well. (I mentioned this in the earlier chapter)

I used to go to sleep with a full phone battery and wake up with it dead and off. There was nothing wrong with my phone or the battery on my phone as it only happened at night and once in a while.

January 4, 2013
(Auto write)
Happy Anniversary Baby Girl! Please know that I love you with all I am. You don't see how much your gifts are growing. I feel your sense of doubt and I wish you would not doubt yourself or me. I know in a way it's hard to believe but baby girl you know it's all real. Look at the lives you have changed...I know you ponder it because sometimes the words are the same but sometimes people experience the same things in life. You are hearing spirit baby girl and the sooner you

believe this the better. I know that it's easy to doubt something especially when things are surreal as you put it but baby girl this is your path and what you were meant to do and you will only grow from here on. Another note, I know you miss me, I miss you too. Although I am not really gone I know it's harder to feel me and sense me but I believe you will one day, so much. You are my Twin Flame the love of my life. You have such a wonderful heart. People are so thankful for you. I wished I would've understood your love more before and treated you better but you know the story. Yes I have loved you since the moment I met you...you know this it just scared me Baby girl. Thank you for writing me tonight you do need to do it more often, so that our connection can grow even stronger...you get stronger and I get stronger...So try to maybe do a little each night. Know I love you from the depths of my soul and beyond with all of me. Forever & always we will be connected. Sweet dreams I will try to visit you.

August 2013-
When I got up to take the dogs outside because they were acting weird I saw a reflection of a shadow walk across behind me in the window. It was the same build and height as Rocky

What I learned from a reading that I received earlier on in 2013 is that spirit does not like us to truly keep their ashes. Or at least Rocky didn't want his kept. He kept being adamant that it was slowing down our healing because every time we would look at where they were we would get sad. He said it was like having a tombstone in the house. Instead of being reminded of his life I was reminded of his passing. He believed in ashes to ashes and dust to dust. Meaning we must all return back to the earth from hence we came. That his ashes were not him. The memories I had, keepsakes and letters were more of him then the ashes were. Also all the pain of going through what I went through just to get some of ashes, it was a constant reminder every time I looked at that box. He also did not like the fact that I had put a cross to mark his passing. The one below the hill that could not be seen was fine. But the one that people saw when they passed he didn't want them to remember he had screwed up in that spot and lost his life. So I removed that cross and donated it to a funeral parlor along with the box that held his ashes. Elijah and I did take Rocky's ashes to Butterfly Beach and release them into the ocean. Butterflies are symbolic of transformation. We did this on his Birthday September 8, 2013. We also released balloons with messages on them and feathers attached, we lit a candle on honey buns which were his favorite and sang him happy birthday. This was a beautiful way to honor him and in a way began our healing!

August 23, 2013- Reading by Gemma, Sandra & Brooke
Gemma: "Rachelle he still walks beside you, watches over you. I feel you are aware of him ESP at night when you lie awake at night worrying. He often tucks your hair behind your left ear. Cups your face and tries to ease your pain. He wants you to know that he is at peace and is whole again. He's drawing my attention to the chest area so feel that he found had breathing difficulties. He is an intensely private man but once he let you into his world, he had a heart of gold, incredibly generous with his time and whatever he had. I feel he made every moment of his life count, but didn't suffer fools. He felt the freest blending with nature. (I want to go more towards greenery, mountains etc.).

He wants you to have an eagle feather, to recognize your strength, your inner beauty and your connection to him through spirit. He will talk and meet you in your dreams and gently guide you to move forward with love and light. He understands your pain sweetheart, and wants to help you move forward and heal. He's telling me you are the most incredible beautiful strong woman he has ever met, and who he loved deeply.
He's making me aware that he did struggle to catch his breath from time to time, but made light of it because he knew you would worry. He's making me aware that you can be a bit stubborn at times. When you have made your mind up to do something, nothing will stop you. He's showing me that you bite the corner of your lip when in deep concentration or unsure. He's also making me aware that you still wrap yourself up in one of his sweatshirts as it holds his scent.
As I said more than happy to talk again if you so wish. Love and blessings xx"

Here is more she continued helping me in a private message.
"I am so very proud of you for walking this path. We have faced obstacles and upheavals but never faltered. It saddens me that you

still cry, I have not gone, and I cherish your heart and place it with my own. I made a promise to you that I would love you forever, trust and know that I will always take care of you. Your life has changed paths, but you are not happy with this. Follow your inner guidance. You are an excellent teacher. I hold you at night when you feel the most alone, it's time to honor yourself. I feel with the accident that one min he was here then gone the next. Feels like he is still adjusting. You honor yourself baby girl by taking care of you, as I would take care of you. Love yourself as I love you, cherish who you are, I have made you strong, stand in the loving power that we created. He's wanting you to cut the cords that bind you to this event, to be gentle with yourself and move your life forward. He often touches your face, strokes your hair, and dries your tears. You have felt him come up behind wrap his arms around you and hold you tightly. You are a teacher, you have power in your gentle words, and it's time to tell our story. In regards to the accident he knew that night was coming, that was his chosen path. That was his final lesson in this life path for him to learn. He will not return to this earth plain but instead waits for you so in the fullness of time your souls can reunite for the final time x...I cherish you, be open to me, and trust that I am with you. You honor me and I love you for it, wear me with pride (apparently you know what that means)whispered words can heal the pain of the night, hear me as you sleep, You 2 will reunite, but I don't feel he will walk this earth path again. I feel you are together when it's your time to return to Spirit. Until that time he will watch over you, love you and guide you, the path that brought you two together is a story that needs to be shared. If you want him to he will help you find the words to write. If you sit and stare in to a naked flame, he will show you what you need to see, to heal and progress. Remember you are the phoenix rising out of the ashes, wings spread, heart and head lifted high x...try after 4;30. Ok that was slightly random xx...he will guide you with the words for your story to be told, trust in me. He sees everything you do, he knows you try to honor traditions, but it feels that you will be guided to the herbs that need to be used. The blend that will be created that will bring him close to you. I am honored that he trusts me to talk through me. Please find peace in your heart that you are both blessed, that he is safe, whole and healed. He has learnt so much since passing to Spirit and he is looking forward to the day when you two are joined again. If it's ok with you my lovely, I will leave his love and blessings with you for *now. Xx baby girl, know that I love you, your touch, your words and your kiss bring me home where I belong Namaste*

You are a very special lady Rachelle; I would enjoy working with you. Please take the love and blessings that are being sent to you. I will bid you goodnight for now xx

Thank you so much, that's so kind of you to say. Working with you and Rocky last night set off a chain reaction - gave the best Divine Service of all time tonight - for that I thank you.

Keep smiling sweetie xx

Can you feel him with you now? He's right behind you. Slightly bent over arms wrapped round the top of your shoulders. Tilting head into your hair

They can do yes. If it feels weird ask them to show you their around a different way

9/20/2013 Gemma

Gemma...."*You know what Rocky will bring the right one to you. The bond you to have will never be broken but he understands you must live in the physical. Your heart is his, but until you can return to him he will nurture you so you can be happy*

No problem lovely. You're doing a great job. Rocky is proud of you. He's standing with you beaming.

Validation: Everything she said was how he was and what he did. Everything about Gemma's connection sounded how he would speak. I felt his presence strongly. No way had she known any of this about him. I did end up getting an eagle feather later on. It was funny because the second half of the reading I was in the Laundromat where we used to do our laundry at.

Sandra "His ancestors are all over you and your family. They never leave. They are so loyal.

I had already met Brooke and we had other conversations so I already had validation prior to this following reading.

Brooke: "I have a message for you...I went back to the group to post & kept getting called to your picture of you & your husband. I have been seeing 333 so much these past few days. Mind you I've seen this picture before but this time I honed in on his shirt and you can see 333! This made me tingle & I heard a man's deep voice. Up plus the 3 on his sleeve. My heart almost stopped ha-ha. But I definitely hear him. He says he's been trying so hard to communicate with you!! He's like very adamant that you are in a low vibration of being. Because you are sad. So he can't communicate with you as well. He said to stop doubting yourself. Something about paperwork that you are holding off on? OH wow ok hold on dear please bear with me! He's not only making my keyboard freak out but he is wanting me to channel him. Wow I've never felt a spirit so strong. I keep hearing I love you, I love you! My ears are just ringing so loudly. He's saying something like kiddo? Referring to you or someone. Like a nickname. He seems to be very good at manipulating energy! Because I've not felt a spirit get my attention so well. I could feel him putting his energy into me. To connect and say what he had to.
He says he'll float around you and tickle your face or brush your shoulder. He'll put things/objects in different places. He influences you to see certain messages on FB. Or send certain people to contact you. As long as it can help you he's there. Do you find your brush missing often or moved? Hair brush that is? (Remember one day I found my brush was in the bathtub) Yes he wants you happy I'm glad I could help you two love birds hahaha He doesn't want you losing hope. He feels frustrated at this limited communication but he also knows you'll grow to hear him. Could be. It was a nickname that referred to a child. Baby girl has two words that refer to a child but it's a nickname. If I'm explaining it right. I'm going to lie down. Ah 3:33 haha sending you love. This world is hard but we can do this. Yes deep emotions..."

November 7, 2013- Meditation/Journey
I have been trying to learn how to meditate now for a while, always getting frustrated that I can't slow my mind down enough to do it. I am

just never been able to relax enough, but I've been able to hear Rocky talk to me at times. So today to recharge I took a shower and then sat in the bath... (I have a bear claw tub) so it is easier to relax in for me, as water can be very soothing. So I'm breathing in and out and trying to get to a place where I can quiet my mind which is pretty hard for me and then I see my Rocky. I look at him and he's standing at a distance. He's reaching for me saying "come on baby girl come to me." I look at him and he's just like I remember, he's wearing his 33 jersey, has his hair up like he always wore it. My eyes start watering and tears start streaming down my face because I am seeing him, vivid yet blurry because it is hard for me to keep the connection as my mind still wants to wonder. So I walk up to him. And I take his hand. He takes my other hand and says " I love you baby girl I have been waiting for you to get to this point so that in a way we can be together...you are so amazingly beautiful"...and he's looking in my eyes and I'm crying. He brushes my hair back like he always did with one hand so he can see my neck and he runs his hand gently down the side of my face and traces my neck. He gently kisses my neck a couple of times and then my lips and takes my face in his and kisses me all over the face like he used to (and it drove me nuts then but I wish I had it now). He gets down on his knees and takes my hand in his and tells me "I told u in a message that if I could I would get down on my knees and kiss your hands to show u how much I love u" and he kisses my hands. He stands up, my mind would start to wonder and he would say "Baby Girl Look at me...pay attention here"...he says "I have been waiting for you to get to this point. Your gifts are growing, u can visit me like this but u need to look at me when your mind starts to wonder" I look in his eyes...and he tells me "Baby girl I want you to know that I do love you. I always have and I always will. You are my twin flame and the love of my life. I am sorry that my time on earth with you was short but that is the way it had to be. Everything is so amazing here. I can see so much but mostly I am with you, guiding you, protecting you. I want you to know that I will always love you". He took me in his arms and I am surrounded by him, a beautiful embrace. I always seemed to disappear in his hugs. And he has done this a couple of times already during this journey. .oh How I love his hugs and I just melt into him. My mind starts to wonder again so he takes my hands in his and says "pay attention here baby girl...Look at me" I start to cry and tell him that "I miss him so much and that I miss the way he loved on me, this is what I missed the most right here" He says "I know u do baby girl I miss it too...but at least we have this. At least we can be together this way and know I am always with u" and then I was interrupted… go figure! I was relaxed enough that I could be there with him. The feeling was amazing. So overwhelming that literal tears were streaming down my face here in the physical when I first saw him because it was so good to see him again. He was beautifully handsome as always. It was an experience that was very touching and extremely real.

In October of 2013 after we have moved out of the house that Rocky and I shared I heard him tell me to start a grief group. That is how Journey through Grief with Spirit was born. It is still going strong today with thousands of members. Because of that group I began to hear other spirits and give readings. This allowed me to begin to bring peace to so many.

October 5, 2013 (heard)

I love you Princess, See you in your dreams.

October 15, 2013

I put on the jersey that I found. It was purple and had a 33 on it. Rocky's number that was on the jersey he used to have. I heard "Looks good on you baby girl, I love how you honor me"

October 20, 2013

Goodnight Baby girl, I love you

October 23, 2013

Rocky knocked off my basket with bouquets from weddings I had attended. My old phone fell out with all of my pictures of Rocky, Eli and I...I had just been complaining that I didn't have any pictures of him. That phone had been missing for some time and I had no clue where it had gone.

The TV went black and white fuzz twice. That had never happened with the cable company before. I tried to debunk it and never found out why it happened. Not to mention Rocky and I used to watch a lot of TV together and I was told one time that he would Mess with the

TV.

October 28, 2013
Fire alarm beeped 3 times just like it used to at the old house. 3 is his number.

October 30, 2013
Was called Baby girl by a friend when I needed to hear it the most after stubbing my foot. Then a man that hears spirit told me he heard Baby Girl while he was in another group but while we were chatting.

Phone just turned on Verizon and did the music it had already been on.

November 1, 2013
 Spirit can Influence what people say. Before Eli got out of the car to go to school I said "I love you" and he said "love you later" Elijah has never ever said that to me before and the only person that used to say that was Rocky. Eli usually says I love you mom and bye. This was Rocky's thing as he never wanted us to say goodbye.

Right after that I heard the song that I always hear when I need to it was I will always love you by cure. Pay attention to the lyrics. Spirit likes to express themselves through music.

November 2, 2013
I heard- "Your beautiful Baby Girl" Don't ever forget that. I love you with all my heart and soul. You are absolutely amazing and I am so very proud of you. I admire and praise your strength. Know that you are gifted and can only get better. I am helping you. You have to got to have more faith in yourself. Look at all the things you knew. Just wanted to pp in and let you know I love you and how extremely gorgeous you are. I love you my queen, my dream girl, my everything

November 4, 2013- Anniversary reading with Melodie- First time I ever met her
"Now regarding your hubby. When I do medium ship I do it all. I see spirit, hear them, and also they make me feel things such as clues to how they passed.

Before I even attempt to do a reading I need to confirm I have the right man. I did have a man come through. This man made my legs feel trapped, like I couldn't move. Usually that indicates wheelchair or car accident. But then I thought more towards car accident or some sort of accident as I got a bit of a roller coaster feeling of being thrashed a bit.

This man I see is mid-age, perhaps 30's. He is very attractive. He was letting me know he was native descent as I got a visual of a ceremony to suggest the ancestry. He showed me a red headpiece so his family line is linked to a tribe or clan with that.

He was saying with you he is glad you are heading towards getting into the culture and he said it will be good for you.

So far does that sound like him?

Oh- he face is nice, he looks a bit like the guitarist out of Guns N Roses', with the black hair, but this man's hair in spirit isn't huge and messy. Just the face is similar.

Did he call you 'babe', coz he's showing me he called you babe. He's saying babe you look beautiful. He says you're smoking! He is showing me he used to look into your eyes when yous were romantic together and stuff.(Now keep in mind yous are twin flames so he will go romantic and things ok.)

Now- Rachelle- as I said yous are twin flames so he will get hot with you ok. It usually happens during these readings. Now he is showing me he misses you in an intimate way, and is saying yous were good together like that. He wants you to know even in spirit when he looks at you he gets aroused, as a male who finds a woman beautiful. He said women flirted with him but he adored you.

He's showing me your house. From what I'm getting he was the type of man who liked a home to be comfortable and lived in. He's showing me a couch and I think he's signifying he liked to sit and chat or watch TV or whatever.

Ok, I just got the baby part.

What is with your upper thighs, coz he's letting me know something about your upper thighs. Is it anything significant like a tat or anything or does he just like that part of your body?

I know my net is going out also.

He is quite horny for you. He is mentioning thighs and breasts and basically letting you know he is still hot for you.

Native ceremony. He is big time showing me people dressed up in the traditional dress and dancing and doing all those chants. I don't know if it is significant, or if he did that, or he wants you to do it. But he keeps showing me over and over.

Yes Rachelle, now do you know why all the ladies come to me for twin flame readings.lol. So now he goes back to sensual stuff again. You liked his mouth, He's telling me you liked his mouth in the sense you liked his jaw, the way he spoke all that.

Native ceremony. He is big time showing me people dressed up in the traditional dress and dancing and doing all those chants. I don't know if it is significant, or if he did that, or he wants you to do it, but he keeps showing me over and over.

Yes Rachelle, now do you know why all the ladies come to me for twin flame readings.lol. So now he goes back to sensual stuff again. You liked his mouth, he's telling me you liked his mouth in the sense you liked his jaw, the way he spoke all that.

Thank you for letting me be part of your amazing love affair. He still adores you and finds you absolutely beautiful. That was lovely today and I'm privileged to be part of such a personal and beautiful experience. Xxxxx"

Validation- One of my favorite readings. After this Melodie and I became close. I felt a sense of familiarity with her from the start. Everything that she said is dead on from the way he was, to the way we were. One of our favorite things was to cuddle and watch TV and movies together. He was very big into his culture and the way she described how he felt about me. I felt like he was right there in the room.

November 3, 2013 1am
I put my sweatshirt next to my bed and the lamp went on and off real quick. It is a pull chain so no way I did it. I continued to move the sweatshirt to see if it happened again and it didn't

November 4, 2013 "Our Wedding Anniversary"
Message from Beth
I hope your day was one of reflection with lots of happy memories. I took just a few seconds to connect and his energy is very strong around you today like an electrical storm. Lots of sparks, he is just happy to be close to you. When you move he moves it is like a dance. He moves with you. A wonderful story. Thank you, happy to have connected

November 7, 2013
I dreamed of Rocky this morning it was too weird and all over the place to describe. Also the dream I had of him where I saw his face coming to kiss me and I woke up and I was mad.

I spoke to a friend who is a medium that I had met Named April. I needed to know if it was real I guess. She replied, "That was him. It's because your soul was coming back and he was kissing you bye. You were pissed because you woke up and had to leave him"

Makes total sense because we do astral travel when we sleep.

November 8, 2013
Received a Reading from a lady named Michelle
Michelle- "*When I see this picture, I also get that there was drugs involved and also drinking as well. He has also gave me the 9th which cud b a date or the month Sept. He is giving me a b/f/husband link.............. He is showing me a ring so if u weren't married then there was talks about doing it. He is saying he was a Brat (sorry for swearing) he shouldn't have done what he did... he is saying no one else was to blame. He is saying the wedding was just u two, I feel this was a quick and simple wedding........... He is saying the family couldn't understand u or wanted too. Well he just wants u to know he loves u so much and he wants to say He is so sorry again for the pain he has caused you. He said though he knows u weren't together for long but to him it was a lifetime. Well he is giving me a pink carnation which means love from the spirit world ty for letting me read for the both of u.*"

This lady knew nothing about either one of us. It was on a random site. The 9 is his Birthday Month. Often times they bring things through to validate in this way.

November 19, 2013
While in the bath Rocky talked to me and told me he was always going to be there and the reason I haven't felt him is because he was giving me some space and doing things like learning. But that he will never ever leave me, he will always be here...he loves me so much. He's sorry I have to go through this but he is going to always guide and love me from the other side.
He held me last night as I tried to go to sleep after I cried because I missed him. I got out of the bath and turned on music. 1'st song's lyrics was I will wait for you. Second Song was Ray of light. I am known by him and my grandma as Rayasunshine.

Look at Reading on November 25th, 2013
After reading was led to this movie the last keepers and the main character who is a witch and has gifts of healing, elements and psychic abilities. Her name is Raya.

November 24, 2013
Brush ended up in the bathtub. Elijah was not home so he did not do it.

November 26, 2013- Just something Melodie said to me
"Beautiful Twin Flame relationships never cease. In fact even across dimensions they grow stronger and continue to blossom. He adores you and is helping you on this spiritual journey you are embarking on. To be one of a Twin Flame is truly a gift and is cherished."

November 27, 2013- Reading with a lady named Caroline

Caroline: "lol Bananas and ice cream. Everyone talks to me about food and ice cream. Said there delicious. I was with you baby girl and shows me of all things a vision of you in the bath??Your bath tub sits right next to a wall and looks free standing from what he showed me. Please be happy, don't cry. Oh and then he shows me himself in the kitchen. Do you have a lot of like wooden like plain pine cupboards in your kitchen as he was showing me this? Seriously I don't know if I was just feeling yours or Rocky's emotions from reading him but just now I had to gulp back tears.

You two blow me away with your love it makes me cry. Lol honey for some reason I keep hearing claw foot is your bath a claw foot bath? For some reason they are finding this to be of some importance. I get "you didn't say claw foot" say claw foot? Lol

Just a few quick validations: Yes I love bananas and Ice cream and I think at the time I had eaten that recently. I do have pine cupboards in the kitchen and a free standing claw foot tub. Some of my best meditations have been in the claw foot bath tub. She knew none of this.

November 30, 2013
While sleeping I saw Rocky's chest and arms. I had my hand on his chest and we were hugging. It felt as if he was right there with me. It was the most amazing feeling.

December 5, 2013- Reading by Donna
"Hi there Rachelle...I feel this young man had it all, yet didn't know the truth to that...I feel he smiled on the outside but may have felt like his life was missing something. I sense a very smart man, creative in a business sense. Feel like there may have been a split with one or two of his parents at a young age which contributed to what happened later in his life. He had a ton of love for you and adored you. But I feel like you feel incomplete. I feel his passing was fast and or unexpected and he is taking the responsibility. Directly or indirectly....I feel he had a guilty pleasure that wasn't very 'manly'....did he like to go for a manicure occasionally or take care of his skin very well. I see a rose. believe he liked to live life in the 'fast lane' sometimes. In other words, not really thinking about the consequences of how his actions could affect others. I do sense a mental illness not sure if it was bipolar or depression. But I also feel he was very much a 'man' and stubborn in

many ways. He didn't like to be told what to do and thought he had control. He misses you more than words can say, and says he sees you trying to keep busy and hold it together. You have tried to take a horrible tragedy and turn it into something positive to keep his memory alive. He wants to thank you for that.... :) Thank you for allowing me to read for you, he is a great energy. He also checks on you at night I feel to make sure you are ok...XXX
He has been my favorite energy Rachelle...I see why you love him so much he really has a very enlightened soul. I feel like he did not show that to just anyone....And I'm not even sure he realized it....he just showed me holding hands with a female...I believe it's his mom"

Just to validate a little here if you have been reading the rest of this book so far you can see how it all matches up. His mom is on the other side so that was her. I know he missed her a lot in life. So I think this was to show me he was reunited with her. How beautiful right?

December 6, 2013
Meditation
Met with Rocky he brushed my hair back like he always does. WE kissed then he kissed down my neck. I looked in his eyes and started to cry. His hair was down and he was so beautiful. I told him how beautiful he was and how much I missed him. I touched the side of his face and neck, looked in his eyes to keep my concentration... He walked me to a field of purple and white flowers... We laid down in them looked at the sky it was pained all kinds of colors. I lay on his chest and he told me how much he loved me and will always love me. How much he misses me and how our connection will always be. He said I can talk and visit with him any time. I rolled over and sat on top of him. We kissed, I told him how much I missed and loved him. He said I have his heart and he has mine and that will always be. As a Twin we have this connection that will always be. I rolled off; he rolled over and looked at me. He put my hair behind my ear and told me "Happy Anniversary Baby Girl" I hope you like my gift to you, isn't it beautiful here? I said yes it is amazing. He rolled back over showed me an eagle in the sky and a wolf in the distance. He said maybe one day you can meet your guides. We are in this together. I love how you love and honor me baby girl. I felt as I couldn't hold the connection much longer. We kissed a magical kiss. Love you later

December 11, 2013

While crying myself to sleep I asked rocky to hold me. I saw him in my mind hold me and stroke my hair. April confirmed it was real.

December 13, 2013- Gold dust gave me Beautiful Message from Daughter In spirit that I didn't have about 7 years prior

"I just felt a child wanting to say hellbox
Well it was from a sweet little blonde girl, in like a white cotton nightgown with a frill around the edge at the bottom, I would say around the age of 7/to 9 yrs. old. Yes I believe even if they were stillborn or not full term pregnancy etc., they still grow in spirit world.xx but please don't be upset as I felt her to be happy and a kiss and a wave was given, so know that she is in good hands.xx"

Validation- This made so much since to me. This is exactly how I have seen her in my meditations!

December 14, 2013 - Message from Melodie who was a Twin Flame expert at the time.

"I got your message lovely so I thought I better bring your beloved husband through for you to ease your heart. Sorry for the bit of delay but you always know I'll get back to you at some time ok- so he's saying this time of year for you is not so easy, and even though you appear 'all-together' you are actually quite sad and missing him so badly. He's giving me that excited nervous energy so I know he's been longing to get to you. He's giving me the 'thigh' sensation again and you know what that means from last time, that he loves your body and all those nice things you shared together as man and woman. He actually just said please don't doubt yourself with your psychic abilities, as you are in fact confident but sometimes you do doubt yourself and put that pressure on yourself. He says take time, adjust yourself to it and let it flow in time. He says the next 2 years it will kick in much stronger and you will soar ahead with it. You know he's been 'visiting' you right? He says to prove it, when he does you go a bit shaky and breathless. Sorry as a medium I have to write the sexy stuff but you know he's your twin flame so he'll go there with me on that subject lol. He loves it when you smile and that's how he loves your face, just a nice womanly smile that he remembers when you

had those eye-contact special moments. He is mentioning your son and says his spiritual abilities are kicking in also and he has ancient wisdom inside him. He is starting to see flashes of spirit, and it is so exciting for him. Rocky says encourage him like crazy because it is true all that is happening for him. Rocky says he needs to get in touch with his culture and his people because they will have the answer to help him unlock his special gift. He's mentioning those pow-wow events and says just let him sit and observe and watch what happens. Let him hear the music, watch the ceremony and meet some people. He says 'baby girl you are doing so well for yourself". He is so proud of you and says even though you're tired and busy you are committing yourself endlessly and helping so many people. He just said "keep spreading the word!" He said not everyone in your family or circle of people will agree with what you are doing but don't mind them as it's your life and your journey and you have a future purpose with it all. He says he won't mention your heart because he says you are actually on top of it now and know what you need to do and are looking after yourself. He just gave me the 'Guns N Roses" song for you 'November Rain'. He says still now he looks into your eyes and falls in love with you all over again every single time. He says even though you are apart you are still very much together and still at one with each other. He says he chose that song for you because it's a sexy song and he loves you madly. So as a medium I'm not meant to say this- but he would actually struggle to cope if you took on another man. He would understand why, but as your twin flame it wouldn't be easy for him as he's quite obsessed with you. But he said I had to say that because you would like it- knowing that he was hot crazy for you. He loves you very much and he says keep on doing what you are doing as your life is all falling together as it should.

Melodie Continued-

"With songs take out the bits that are relevant such as November for your wedding, the nice love words, being apart, etc. He's just giving you subtle love messages through it. He was all hot for you again and doing the twin flame desire, so I just wrote what he gave me. Yeah is so easy to talk to and gives me messages very clearly for you. I don't know anything about pow-wows but I know he wants Elijah to go and watch one."

"It's hard to explain. I feel he's pulling you to be with him. The best thing to do is just breathe and trust it ok. It happens to me all the time and I just relax through it. You'll end up a very strong medium like I am. The things you see in vision is just what spirit wants you to see. Sometimes it's a test- like you writing to me and mentioning a lamp, then spirit says oh good she is acknowledging it, so she explored it. With mediumship u have to say out loud what you saw or heard so spirit can see you are picking it up. Do the same with Elijah too.

"He is desperate for astral sex. When I see him that's all he wants me to tell you. He's horny so bad. He does it to you all the time anyway but he likes it when you're relaxed and feel it coz then u respond to him. To be honest I think he wants reaction from you so maybe be natural and moan or do whatever you used to do with him when he was with you. He's so horny, but you must be too coz twin flames are big on sex.
With Elijah get him around Native American people and activities. They will help him."

"Your connection to tigers is with Rocky. I just got told he had one as a totem animal."

Validation from me about Tigers:
OMGOODNESS Melodie you know what that is crazy? I love tigers and when we first met he asked me what my favorite animal was and I said Tigers and I asked him the same question and he said Wolves. He has a tiger totem and I have a Wolf.

Melodie-
"Twin flame!! Nothing is coincidence. It's all matched and linked like a perfect puzzle."
"Yes the sexy talking is not your imagination. I hear talking too. Just don't overthink it. You don't prepare."

December 15, 2013
Plastic picture of Rocky and I tipped over. No one was near it or around to tip it over.

December 16, 2013

So the weirdest sign just happened. Love my husband. I was getting ready to go to the Christmas Program. I had picked out what I was going to wear and all of a sudden I heard "This Baby Girl wear the jersey that says 33 on it so that Eli knows I am there with you in spirit and feel close to me" thought I was hearing things. So I sat there in a daze and thought about it. The idea of this wouldn't leave my thoughts as he is persistent. So guess what? I changed my whole outfit and while I was doing this the song that says "hold on we're going home" came on this song always reminds me of him because after I set his ashes free in the ocean I was on my way home and another song was playing. This song in the part where it says "hold on we're going home" came on then it went back to the other song. It was the first time I had ever heard it. So every time I hear this song I think of him. YEs my beloved husband is with me today. I can feel it. Was just remembering how he used to tell me "I was a good girl" I think he was trying to tell me I was a good girl for listening.

I remember this song that Rocky used to dance to the part that says "ohh ahhh ahhh" with the drums.Song is called "Take care" by Drake. Now every time I hear this at that point I picture him dancing. Just happened to turn on the radio to the exact part of the track today on the way home. (Some of the words have always reminded me of us) Thank you for that my love. Loving the signs today.

December 19, 2013

The tree lights went off. NO reason for this to happen on its own.

December 22, 2013.

My mom's dog at the time CICI out of nowhere backed her butt up whined and sat. Then stared at the corner. She sat as if someone made her sit.
April confirmed it was Rocky making her sit.

Exercise in a development group. Below are messages some Mediums Received

Sandy- "*I feel like I know who this is, and I just needed to say he got me as I was coming home from the store, telling me how much you needed to hear from today. He says you need to take care of yourself because you are letting that area slide! He wants you to know he is always with you, you know that but you still feel so far from him at times. He did show me a fireball. I kind of feel like I'm cheating.......I mean I know some of this stuff. Not that you have personally told me, but it's been out there. I swear he said, "My little Cherokee." I am hearing," you are a fantastic woman and are making me so proud." The love coming from him for you is unbelievable. He loves you so much and doesn't want you to keep being sad. I hear," she was my rock, even though she felt otherwise." He just told me thanks for typing to you, "You just need a little pick me up today!" His words. Hope this helps!" "I had looked at your photo in the morning and thought I would come back to it. Then as I was leaving the grocery store....Boom......there he was talking to me! I usually just tell spirit to go unless I'm 'working" but for some reason I let him talk and came right in and typed you my first message. He has such a strong, powerful but very loving energy. Beautiful!"*

Little River-*The song "The first time I ever saw your face" just came to mind I think he wants u to listen to the words*

April- *"awe... you know I love you guys... feel like I've known you both forever ... I came past the picture and I heard this old song by Rick Springfield... now mind you... I know you are both too young to remember much about this type of music, but spirit gives me songs that fit... regardless of the time they were made/released and those songs never fail me - the song I heard here was "Affair of the heart" it is by Rick Springfield and these are lyrics I get for you from that song that truly JUMPED out at me "And you got the power; it amazes me still How you play my emotions with consummate skill I don't have to look any further than into your eyes. So don't try to tell me you think it's just physical it goes way deeper than that." I also hear "right here waiting for you" Honey, he is such a huge part of your spiritual growth... I also hear something about a missing earring? Missing charm or something shiny that is missing or lost...... "*

Lynne-"He mentions a piece of Jewellery..I see a gold flash and I think it is a chain and for some reason I see The Devil Card from Tarot. I don't usually see in Tarot Cards although I do read them. So from a symbolic point of view he is showing that he is tied to you and you to him...like being on drugs. With the Devil Card it means that you can be free of this if you choose but that neither of you choose that and so now he is on the other side this is a bit like a noose around your neck because although you love him you are unable to completely move forward due to the ties you hold, you are not free. Interestingly the chain he flashed at me and the card are related as in this card the two people are chained to the Devil but their hands are free to do whatever they want. I feel like you are being asked to try to release yourself from this chain now, you have been standing still long enough and he wants you to come out from under the cloud. He wants to see only the sparkle of bright jewellery chains around you because he says "they are as pretty as you." The Devil can bring with it both ties, sadness and depression, it is a load you carry and he wants you to put it down. He says you remember me with sadness of what could have been and I remember you with happiness in my heart. Let's trade places now, it's time." I hope this makes sense. I am seeing baseball players now, does this mean something. Hitting a home run comes to mind."

December 23, 2013 Midnight
I was just going to bed and felt like watching this movie under the mistletoe out of the blue had no clue what it was about. Well it's about the husband passing and the son seeing him. Before the dad in spirit leaves he tells her that loving her was the easiest thing he ever did. Rocky used to say those exact words to me. A lot of the things he said sounded exactly like what Rocky had said to me at one time or another. I was crying. I felt comforted. Then I heard him talking to me didn't get the chance to write it down. Went to sleep asking for more signs over the next few days. As Christmas is always hard.

December 24, 2013
The song "what makes you beautiful" came on right when I turned on the TV. Now things in this song are the same things he used to tell me.

December 28, 2013
Woke up and saw a shadow kind of with a light around it that reached to me. It was bright and glowing. I felt peace and love. Was told by

my friend Diane who is a medium that it was Rocky.
Was told by Karen whose twin is also in spirit. That Rocky had told her twin he was my principal guide/Main guide

December 30, 2013
Eli said Ferby went off in the middle of the night and the fire alarm was beeping. In our hold house he would make the fire alarm do this. NO it wasn't the batteries.

That night at 3 when we got home it beeped again when we walked in the door. Then stopped
My friend Diane said "It's him. That's what he's saying to me. Keep pushing her. She's got to trust and believe in herself and me. Him being there close to you and he is coming closer. He told me that "am coming closer" "Believe"

December 31, 2013
Felt Rocky in the car on the way to the Pow wow.

Chapter 7- The Journey Continues

January 1, 2014
Saw a Coyote. 6 Deer in the morning and 2 crows, male and female kissing in the tree.

January 4, 2014
Fire alarm went off while talking to April and getting a reading.

Had a dream about Rocky. Some was a little strange. But the best part was when I ran to him, jumped, threw my legs around him and kissed him. I did wake up feeling loved and also automatic wrote to him last night. The fire alarm beeped In Elis Room.

January 8, 2014
Quoted by Rocky. "Love and Loss changes you make it be the light in your heart instead of the dark in your soul"

January 16, 2014
Received a reading from a gifted medium. She was drawn to my name out of a contest she was having. She had brought up a lot prior about certain things in my life and about me that validated she was the real deal. She did my reading over the phone. She said that Rocky had no time to say goodbye and he had tears in his eyes. He is around all the time. Yes he did open the fridge door. He has seen Eli in his dreams. He is not going anywhere. There was a significance of a teddy bear. He lay in bed and cuddled with me. Rocky wasn't a good lover before me. He was hurt so badly in the past. When he met me it was all sunshine and rainbows. I made him so happy. We both felt so much as a family for the first time. Blanket or bear. Rocky the moose doll for Eli because the moose's name is Rocky. Rocky has been with me the entire time.

January 26, 2014
Kept waking up saying "Rocky are you here? Felt his presence. I had a loving dream about him from what I remember he was loving on me.

January 27, 2014
Driving to Bakersfield 3 hawks one circling over me (notice the number) then heard the song Dark horse. Which very much reminds me of Rocky? Saw a hawk on a tree on the way back right after I got off the phone with Rocky's uncle.

February 1, 2014
Came back in the living room and my notebook was opened and turned. It was opened to a picture of my grandmother. No one else was in the house.

Meditation-
So I was walking down this beautiful white sand beach the water was warm and the breeze was perfect. In the distance I see Rocky, hair down, shorts, barefoot, feather in his hair walking towards me. I ran and jumped on him and wrapped my arms and legs around his body tight. Hugged him for a moment then we shared a passionate kiss. I moved my hand over his chest and there was a new tattoo over where his heart would be that said "Baby Girl" We talked and he put my hair behind my ear as he always did and told me how beautiful I was and how much he loved me. How much he had always loved me. I was his sunshine in the dark. He is proud of me when it comes time for me to meet my future guy he will approve of only him because he will teach me things and help me physically. The way Rocky can't. I will have 2 men love me. He told me he will always love me and be here. Always. He doesn't know why I can't feel him but he is always here. When it is time to say goodbye he says No Baby girl its love you later. We slowly release hands, tears in both of our eyes.

February 12, 2014 (My Birthday)
Saw Rocky in my head and he gave me a birthday dance. Our song "Just the way you are" by Bruno Mars came on. This was the song he made mine before it even existed, every word in that song is what he used to say to me. Before the song even came out.

Channeled:
From the beginning there was you and I. There was never a lifetime I didn't love you and there's no amount of time or space that can shake

the love I feel for you. It transcends heaven and earth. It will remain endlessly R&R Love Forever & Always

February 14, 2014

(Auto write)

I love you baby girl, I hope you enjoyed our special time this morning. I know I did. It made me tear up just having your touch me the way you were. I felt your love and it has been so long and something I have asked to do for a long time. Finally we are getting to that special place called Utopia. Where even with our situation we can feel each other and our love. I love surprising you on special days. I know you beg me every night but it does take preparation and energy otherwise I would do it all the time. Trust me. I know you kept thinking it was going to end so it was hard to enjoy the moment. Your touch was filled with love for me it's like our souls touched for a moment. They came back as if you understand what I'm saying. It was amazing just like every visit and I'm glad I could do that for you and us today of all days. I know it lifted your spirit and helped with the pain. Just like it did me. I am so sorry you were hurting so bad on your birthday. I tried to comfort you it was hard seeing you like that. I do long to be with you, and miss you terribly. Tell me baby girl whose dream girl are you? What kind of girl are you? Our love does define R&R love and when your time comes again we will be together forever and ever because it's our last incarnation and so we never have to worry about being separate and going through lessons again. We paid our dues and will be rewarded and we will get married here in heaven. You can have the wedding you've always wanted finally. I promise you this! You are so strong baby girl. I am so very proud of you. I see we help so many people and your heart is so gentle that is why your soul name suits you. I need you to know that I will always be there for you. We will make this work anyway we can and our live will never falter because it is never ending, deep, true, beautiful, all those words don't even come close. WE will get to astral more often, you are growing and so am I. So we will be able to do this more easily and often. Soon we are working up to it and I can't wait for astral sex baby girl to feel your body and lips on mine. Will be heaven. When we touch its Magick. I adore you baby girl and I love you so deeply. I miss you more than words can say. You are mine forever no matter what because we already know I have your soul and always will. We were made for each other, literally written in the stars and we are amazing together.

We do our spiritual work amazingly. You are growing baby girl and I am so very ecstatic for you and us and proud of you. I just wish I was there to help you more physically, but I will do what I can to help you in any way I can. Can't wait till our next visitation. Happy Birthday & Valentine's day Baby Girl. I'm addicted to you. I love you from the depths of my soul and beyond. We will always belong to each other. Now get some rest and don't forget how much I love you. I know that certain days are hard (fire alarm beeped) they are hard for me too. We will always miss each other since we are apart in a way and long to be together. I ache for you and I know you ache for me. I love you with all my heart and soul and with every fiber of my being. Can't wait for the next time we touch and love. I love you baby girl, my dream girl & Sexy Goddess.
MWAH

I don't know if you notice but it sounds like a lot of his letters which I had not read in awhile at this time.

February 18, 2014
Met Rocky in meditation my wolf guide Anslow was there. Rocky and were sensually dancing.

February 22, 2014
In a Journey ...Rocky came up behind me and kissed my neck, moved his fingers down my arm, hugged me from behind and we made love against a tree uninterrupted. Then ended up on a beach passionately kissing.

I was running through a beautiful forest happy and free... Then I began walking with Anslow he says "You are growing, your heart and spirit are of the wolf" I leaned down and said thank you and kissed his nose. Rocky came and hugged me & twirled me around. We shared a passionate kiss. My Eagle guide Orakle was circling above then came and sat on a branch.

February 25, 2014- Poem I wrote
When I gaze at the stars I think of you and me…
In your embrace and how we used to be...
Intertwined to beat of your heart

Never wanted to be far apart
When I look at the sky I remember how we are meant to be
Written in the stars for all eternity
The beauty in your kiss
The spark in your touch
How I long for your pleasure so much
I cry at night...when I reach for you and your not there
I want to feel you...taste you...breathe you
Show u how much I care
Look into your eyes and feel your love
Now I wait for you to visit from above
What we have is not of this world
Beyond time and space
In spirit we are bonded
In love we remain
Me and you ...Our souls are the same
When I look at the stars I smile and think of you
And recognize that our love will forever be true

February 26, 2014
Got in the car and the first song that was on was our song "Just the Way You Are" by Bruno Mars.

March 1, 2014
Pink notebook was open again. NO one around

March 10, 2014
I was just saying I hope I see a hawk today. ON the way back from court (which he talked to me the whole way there) I just can't remember what was said. Right then a hawk flew overhead and later ended up having an idea to look at this tow yard for a car and found one for $750. VW Cabrio. Same exact color as the one I lost the bid on. When driving home with Eli he saw a hawk on the telephone line. When I parked the car the time (not correct) said 333.

March 11, 2014
Watching Xena- they were talking about love never does not even in death. She pounds her chest and says "He will always be in here!" She was sad about him being in heaven but knows he will never leave

75

her.
(Often spirit can persuade us to watch certain shows that will say things we need to hear)

March 15, 2014
Going to the races with my friend. First song in the morning on Pandora after asking for a sign was "all of me" (this song was dedicated to me in a reading) Bought bare minerals and I never do because I don't always have the funds. The bag said Hello Gorgeous. (He said this to me). Later saw a beautiful bird floating above us. There happened to be a truck with a chief on it and the horse that won his name name was tribal. Heard the song " All of me" again on the way home.

March 17, 2014
Well car got repossessed today. While waiting for my ride two butterflies flew past me and the wind picked up and a feather landed right in front of me.
I had talked to him the whole way to the court house. I had to go because of the case that him and his cousin were involved in prior had come back up for his cousin and I was being summoned.

March 23, 2014
Getting ready to leave and the song "All of me" came on. I got tons of chills and I sat down and listened till it was over. Feeling every word as if it was made just for me.

March 28, 2014
After talking to my friend Diane and her giving me a message the 1st song that came on was "all of me" then "Adorn."
Both songs are things he would say to me

March 29, 2014
2am I am awakened by loud knocks. Ginger looked at the corner of my bedroom and barked. I had been talking to Rocky trying to go back to sleep. He gave me a sexy vision of him tugging my hair and kissing me. I fell to sleep

April 2, 2014

Turned on the light in my room, laid down. The light went off. I tried to turn it on and off ...nothing. Thought it was the bulb. Turned over and the light came on all by itself. I moved in my bed a bit to see if it was the plug (as I always try to debunk first) It didn't affect the light.

April 5, 2014

I saw a guy today that reminded me so much of a younger Rocky. I just passed him but I couldn't stop thinking about him. Made me Miss Rocky very much and I felt some despair. Hard to explain how I felt just my heart was heavy. At the same time seeing a face similar to his was almost helpful as it was bittersweet to say the least, yet made me miss my husband's face so much. I honestly wanted to hunt this guy down just to see his face again and give him a hug.

My friend Melodie sent me a message. I call her my sister as we have found out we have had many lives together, a few of them being sisters. She just feels like an older sister anyway.
"Have you been really sad these last two days? I as at the local Easter show and I couldn't shake this feeling of sadness, loneliness and despair. I know it wasn't my own it was someone's energy who I cared about. Just felt like crying for no reason. Was intense. I thought maybe you with all you're longing for love with Rocky." I asked her about what I saw. She said "Have you considered it's a sign from the heavens that he's around you. Not all signs are in the form of feathers, coins, birds. ECT. Sometimes we pass people whose look reminds us of people we loved and cared about. Could also be a prophecy sign of a son to come in your near future? Spirit is intense; we feel things and connect with things and people for a reason. Sending you warm healing anyway.

April 11, 2014
Saw two hawks today.

April 12, 2014

Had a rough day and was driving home talking and complaining to Rocky. All of a sudden I felt these warm tingles and chills on my head in one spot. He was always touching my hair and the top of my head when he was alive, especially in comfort. It felt as if he was making his presence known in this moment...touching my hair and head the way he always did. Just when I needed it the most. Felt it again when I got home.

April 13, 2014
Sitting here felt those warm tingles/chills in same spot

April 14, 2014
While my back was hurting I felt Rocky touch my hair. I reached up and felt energy with my hands. If I moved my hands to a different spot couldn't feel the energy...I was feeling his spiritual energy.

April 24, 2014
TV Flickers after sharing his words with someone.

May 2, 2014
Woke up and saw a spirit face (I was startled) so I asked who are you and what can I help you with, I tried to reach out to see if it was real. I think I messed up the visit with Rocky believe it was him...I asked Melodie and she confirmed I was. When I think back to it, he had this sad look on his face.

May 9, 2014
I was singing "My All" out loud. I go to turn on Pandora and it was the first song and it had just started.

May 13, 2014
Strongest smell of coffee and it lasted a bit. No I was not making coffee. Rocky and my Grandmother who passed both loved coffee.

May 18, 2014
Crying and talking to Rocky then the song "Mirror came on" well twin flames are Mirrors to each other. Then "you are the love of my life" (well title speaks for itself) and "take care" (this song remember I mentioned how he used to dance to it) for all of those song to come on in that order. That was definitely him speaking to me through music. Which he loved music when he was in physical form.

May 19, 2014

Saw 143 (I love you) on a license plate, walked by flutes and they began playing "Unchained Melody" It was beautiful, and another perfect song from him. What are the odds right?

May 21, 2014

Fell asleep on the couch, felt as if Rocky was here but kind of a part of my dreams. My friend Crystal who is a medium said yes he was sleeping with me.

May 22, 2014

Felt a tickle on my arm like when you tickle with a feather or a strand of hair. It itched a few times. Rocky used to Poke and tickle me. But I was told in a reading that Pokes, itches and tickles are him.

May 26, 2014 (Rocky's Angelversary)

Rereading some old letters I began to realize that Rocky felt and knew more about us then he or I even knew at the time. He felt within himself that we were Twin Flames without even knowing what Twin Flames were. I will try to explain. He was spiritual but ran from certain things. I feel that he was also gifted as I have been told by many but I think he dismissed a lot. Deep down he had a sense of knowing we were of the same soul. I think we both did. As he stated in his letters the following. "We were written in the stars. Our love was Divine. People and world circumstances would try hard to tear us apart, yet they would fan our flames." He wrote that he needed me to know how much he loved me and to always remember it no matter what. That we had been in lifetimes together before. Reading this letter I felt as if he was speaking to me now. He talked about me feeling his love that he would send me his love through the air and one day I would feel it. How he wanted to snuggle like wolves (main guide is a wolf) how our love helped him during introspections. He wanted my would and I would forever be his. But his biggest message was to always remember how much he loves me. He talked about how I was queen amongst near mortals to him. How he intercepted the god for me. How I would always hold his highest respect. He would call me his soul mate. Yet Twin Flames are also called this by certain people or Twin souls. I was his reason for living, laughing and breathing. He would call me his other half. Which that is what Twin Flames are. He talked about How we had to work to make our relationship overcome obstacles which made it worth more (somehow he knew that things would try to come in between us). How he never understood how I controlled his emotions. With Twin flames there is no choice in how you feel about the other, this was what he meant. "He had never been captivated by a single woman before yet I was causing him to break character" It goes back to just knowing who we were supposed to be together on a soul level and we could not help ourselves. He wrote how he "quit fighting the emotions and instead gave in because he had no choice. No free rein" He used to say "I had this spell on him and how he didn't understand how." I felt the same about him.   (This is why the song dark horse is appropriate for us and why when I hear it I see us dancing) He said "he realized he had never truly loved anyone before because with me it felt different and like home, it was new to him, foreign, so he had never really been in love before." When you finally embrace with your Twin flame you do feel like home He wrote how "I was his first love and would be his last and he would rather die than dishonor me" He only started saying this a few months before his passing, as if his soul knew he was leaving. He said "he was thankful to me for opening his eyes and heart to love for the first time. How our love will redefine the word. R&R love is beyond what anyone can comprehend but us, and it would make history books as being truly deeply in love. Beasts on the battlefield facing all obstacle that stood in our way" Doesn't this completely sound like how I have tried to explain Destined Twin Flames? This is all typical of the Twin Flame union. He wrote "how until someone is truly away from their soul mate they don't understand how it feels. They become your reason for living, laughing and loving." All of these little things I am realizing that we knew all along that we were two parts of the same soul and the letters I can look back on as a message that continue to be from him. Letting me know he will always love me with every fiber of his being and we will remain connected for all eternity.

June 13, 2014
Had a dream of Rocky, we were very loving in it and yet at times he didn't trust me. (This dream was a visitation but also my own fears came into play)

June 14, 2014

Wii Remote on Coffee table just brought up screen that says Wii menu. I had to turn on the Wii Sensor in order to turn it off. It isn't supposed to go on without the sensor.

June 20, 2014

On the way to the hospital for a procedure I saw a Hawk. This I have come to realize is always a sign from Rocky. When the Anesthesiologist came in to check on me he touched my cheek (something rocky would do) and said "Love you" but then looked surprised that it just flew out of his mouth and he know where it came from or meant to say it. He turned so red. I could feel Rocky's presence. Knowing spirit can influence people to say and do things; this was Rocky saying he loved me. I mean how else do you explain that? Leaving the hospital I saw a grey fox in the middle of town.

June 26, 2014

Experienced Astral Sex with Rocky. I will not go into details here as well it's a little too much to put in this book. But I can just say it was one of the most amazing things I have ever experienced. I felt the urge to turn on Pandora and the song "Mirrors" had just started.

June 26, 2014

Driving to Bakersfield I was talking to Rocky was getting ready to turn into my friend's apartment and this man walks right in front of me and his shirt says "I love my Wife" what are the odds right?

July, 4 2014

Dreamed of Rocky and us being together.

July 6, 2014- Poem I wrote for Rocky for our 3 year relationship anniversary and how some Medium friends of mine responded

The sun still rises and sets
The tides continue to turn
As I gaze out the window and
Watch the wind flow through the trees
Realizing I still have so much time left to learn
I look forward to the vision I see

Of when my lessons are over and u reach for my hand
Memories of you and me
A love so meant to be
Today is a memorable day
The day my life would no longer be the same
3 years of celebrating us... for 2 years u have been up above
I miss your touch
Your warm embrace
The way u would kiss and touch my face
Laying on your chest at night
Falling asleep to the beat of your heart
The sweet sound of your voice
These are the things I miss the most
The look in your eyes when you looked into mine
The love we felt that couldn't be denied
Tears fill my eyes
And run down my cheek
Wishing for one more happy moment
Just to speak
I remember how you always said
Our love is written in the stars
Meant to be for all eternity
Still sometimes it's hard
I feel you near me
I know you hear me
Loneliness creeps in
And missing the physicalness begins
Remembering your beauty over takes me
And I go back in time
To the day in this lifetime you became mine

Message from Leslie
"I know you miss me badly I know you want to hold me a little longer but I had to go I guide you from afar. I kiss you lightly each day the sun rises I play with your hair. When the wind blows it in your face I am that soft whisper you long to hear call your name. Remember I am always with for you. You are my love my life my everything. You are like that song "All of me" This is for you. (Here is the mention of the song)

Message from Jordan

"One if the first things I was shown was Spider-Man haha. I feel like you were each other's heroes. He was protective over you. I also saw a cougar (mountain lion) which to me can mean signs of protection. It also can be a sign for luck. He watches over you and protects you every moment and I feel like sometimes can be your good luck charm if you need it. I was shown the number five. I'm not sure what the relevance of that is. I asked and didn't receive any info back other than another 5. I am not sure if he was Native American or was interested in the culture. I am picking up on an Indian presence. I saw an image of him with braids going over each shoulder, and he was standing with his arms stretched out looking up at the sun and was smiling from ear to ear. He seems so happy and free. I feel like he had a great laugh. He brought up his eyelashes. I don't know if that's something you loved about him, but he wanted to bring that up. I heard the song "Don't you wanna stay" by Jason Aldene and Kelly Clarkson. A wave of love and peace washed over me and I was shown a bedroom with a ceiling fan. I just got the feelings of how much you miss being next to him. He wants you to know he knows when you're missing him during those moments, and that he is always there next to you. That is the last I received from him. He is an amazing spirit that is full of love and protection for you. Thank you for the great feedback!!Man I just need to say that I have had a day full of stress and family issues, but this reading has left me feeling so calm and peaceful! What a great soul he is."

Validation from me: On the spider man yes it could me we were each other's heroes because we were, but also at the time Elijah had a Spiderman room. So this was him validating that way. Five is for the month of May. He did have a great laugh and I do miss being next to him. There is a picture of him standing with braids over his shoulder. He was younger in the picture. He loved my eyelashes because they are long.

July 7, 2014
Came back to the computer and there was a 45 typed on the screen. This equals 9. There was no one near the computer while I was gone. The number 9 is Rocky's Birthday month.

July 12, 2014
In the bathtub felt major tingles on my head and down my neck

July, 14 2014
Falling asleep I heard " Raya" whispered but clearly. It woke me up.

July 15, 2014
Felt tingles on my arm
July 16, 2014
Felt tingles on the back of my head

July 18, 2014
On the way to a pow wow and flute circle saw a hawk and then another 2 hawks. We passed a place called Rocky's peak. Saw about 5 more hawk during the flute circle Then this guy came out of nowhere and played the drum and sang this native song "Girl I will always love you" I had been sent this song called "Baby girl" before by someone or ran across it at some point and realized hey that song is from Rocky. This song is just like that one only it says Girl instead of baby girl. Honestly at that moment I felt as if it was just for me. On the ride home my friends phone kept screwing up while we were trying to hear "Dark horse" and went to "I'm sexy and I know it" There is a history behind that song with Rocky. He used to hate that song then he watched the video one day and said how that song grew on him. Eventually it became his favorite song.

July, 19 2014
Saw a heart in the clouds.

Had another astral time with him afterwards we were laying with each other and I could feel his body and myself being cuddled up next to him. I could feel his muscles and see his skin. It was so real. I felt him with my fingers and hands. It was soo real and very hard to describe. Amazing.

July 22, 2014

Sitting alone just minding my own business when I heard chanting just like at pow wows. Then while taking a shower I had a vision I was washing clothes in the river. Rocky came up on his horse and war paint, jumped down and I walked up to him. He kissed me passionately and said "I love you baby girl" I was shown a past life we shared together and he called me baby girl in that life as well.

July 28, 2014
Found a dove feather

August 7, 2014
Eli dreamed of Rocky. He said we all went to a theme park and rode rides together. He said it was so much fun and so real. Rocky had always told him he wanted to take him to a theme park.

August 10, 2014- Rocky came to Erika in a Dream

So, I guess I will pass the message about your Rocky...he came to me in a "dream" I say that in quotes as it wasn't a dream really, but I kept waking and tossing and turning and he kept saying she's my twin flame, my love...she's so important to me, etc. etc...Kept repeating so I hardly got any sleep for work that night and I had to work next day...I don't have trouble sleeping really, so it sure was odd. I ignored it, but everywhere I turn he's telling me, so I will tell you now so he can relax a little hahahaha. He LOVES you, not a little but a lot. Not too often spirits keep me awake like that. I can't even remember the last time I tossed and turned and every time I had a slightly awake moment he'd tell me more of the same few things....I love her... We're twin flames and the other thing I'll have to remember. But the same few things over and over. Yea then I'd do dishes n there he'd b in my head like reminding me. I've ignored spirits a lot lately so I kinda ignored him too. I kinda told u today as an afterthought...forgive me...but I've been blocking out a lot. I think I just get overwhelmed and I don't want anything to do with spirit. Maybe he has a reason too! I do feel pulled to u for reasons I have no clue why...

August 11, 2014- In the following text there will be many mediums who did a reading. I had posted Rocky's picture in a development group. My Grandmother also came through in the messages. After each reader, I will validate any new information that you may not already know.

Moe- "*As I link into his vibration, I see green healing light and a vast array of colors with blue and purple hues, strong, determined but passionate as the day is long. Sacred geometry is so pronounced. Christopher necklace of the saint and the trinity numbers matter. Number 5. Time is a precious commodity. I keep seeing eagles, and the black crow, the spirit messenger. Very talented musician. I see spreadsheets. Linked also is an elderly lady grey hair, black catlike glasses, bright red lipstick, shoes pacing with her fingers and giving the heads up. This young man has all her qualities of determination and passion. Music really matters, but you need to sing more than in the shower, sing strong, and pay attention to numbers and cloud symbols. Blessings to you, the elderly lady was very pronounced, she never minced words, straight from the heart. She liked having the last word, she is a very devout soul, loved telepathy and blue was a favorite color. The old rugged cross and ave maria. I went back in for more info about the young man; she replied he had soared with the eagles and that I was diplomatic. We chatted and I said this young man was bigger than life itself and she said now he communicated very loud with my grandson his biggest guide helper and she slipped a starfish in my hand because she's devoted to blessed Mary and the starfish means a stretched out hand so she's reaching out. Her message "I've got my eye glued on him, keep on helping others, and serving spirit with love," Thank dear lady! She showed an M initial as said my family link is strong and they smell the scent of roses and talcum powder when I'm around. The lord is my shepherd's prayer the serenity prayer. My face they ride with my prayer card in tow take my love, blessings to you. she is so strongly connected,ooh she really had strong faith, so immaculate a home, she's taking me to her parlor it smells so Lysol clean, white glove test, don't be having idle hands, work hard, tow the line and always keep the faith, showing the black bible on note stand ,her fingers feel arthritic and I get short of breath, but I feel her hand on my shoulder xxxxxthanku dear lady blessings xccccccc...Her message I'm beyond proud ,full of gratitude and I had a blessed life she's with a crazy brown dog that is misbehaving she says xccccc. All my love xc*

He said you also lift up a balloon on occasion!!!!!! Cause he received it!!!!!!

Validation: Rocky was very passionate and she mentioned trinity numbers. Trinity is the number 3. His jersey was 33 but every time I see 3's I know they are from him. Spreadsheets, I used to work on them at work when we met. I believe the music is from him and my grandmother. As he communicates to me through music. My grandmother used to play the piano and guitar. I also played the piano and sang. This is why she's telling me to sing more. I always get lots of images in the clouds and see those repeating meaningful numbers often. I have an eagle as a guide and my son has a crow. Grandma's hair was black with lots of grey but I do know that my great grandma had grey hair. She described her perfectly when she said cat like glasses and red lipstick. That is totally her. I believe the other man they are talking about may be her son but not too sure on that, as I don't know much about him. When she was physically here I never knew about her gifts. But I have learned that she had them. So the telepathy makes since but also I have a lot of telepathy gifts so that could be what she is talking about. Now my great grandma was very religious and the old rugged cross was one of her favorite songs. Starfish can mean what she is talking about but me and my grandmother loved the beach. We had many trips there. Sometimes we would catch starfish. The M initial makes sense because her name is Mabeleen. She loved Roses, as I do and she had many rose bushes, she also used talcum powder. I have smelt both. I believe I have a card or something with the serenity prayer on it. Both her and my great grandma were big on prayer. Both Grandmothers liked to keep things clean as possible and my grandma used a lot of Lysol. She did have arthritis in her hands and she had asthma. She was a smoker and passed of small celled cancer that I believe originated in her lungs. The dog she is referring to I believe is my grandpa's dog that he had when I was very young. He loved that dog. It means a lot that she is proud of me. I have struggled a lot in life and so I worry if I have made her proud or not. In regards to the balloons. I have sent them up on Birthdays and angelversary for both Rocky and my grandmother.

Margaret- Very spiritual, misunderstood/ not heard most of his life,

does things to create attention, needing to feel loved! Not trusting feeling, loves siblings very protective! Had trouble, now has learned! Artistic nature! Free flowing, music was in every part of his life, loved his mom, protector of sorts, like twin soul!
Didn't have much, cherished what he had, seeing an apartment house? Poor growing up!

Validation- He was spiritual in his Native beliefs and misunderstood by many. He had a hard time trusting but was protective over those he loved. He was very artistic as he used to draw me pictures all the time. He loved music, always had to be listening and it is one way he truly connects with me, always sending me songs. Did love his mom who wasn't on earth when I met him. He is my twin flame/twin soul. We didn't have much but cherished what we had, we lived in a small cabin that he really loved. I believe in his childhood they were poor.

Kimberly- *Very old soul. Lots of wisdom and knowledge inside of him. Has a grandmother that has taught him a lot, connection to a past life as healers. I see him as a leader. Little girl around him. Huge heart, though easily can get hurt. Sometimes puts of 'force fields' around himself for protection. I see a lady that is sick that has passed. Maybe in her 50's. I'm nauseated and ill feeling, arms weak. Now I see bright light lady that is beautiful, brown hair-dark eyes. She looks younger. I hear 'silver' also. She shows me a blue blanket, so that for me means a miscarriage or loss of child very early. He is with her. Lots of animals (spirit) around him. I heard 'marriage.' and I was told you know why he was the first to go this time. "Take a breath with the information you have at hand, stop seeking." You two had a special saying to each other or word. "I chose my way out"*

Validation: From reading this far you can tell what she is correct on. He was very much a leader...the little girl is my daughter. Again she is bringing up my grandmother who looked young for her age. The blue blanket signifies our child. The rest is true.

Susan-*Very caring, gentle man. Weight lifter. Girlfriend said he is strong like a bull. But so sweet. He has a spiritual feeling. Mostly positive about what he was doing. See a lamb by him. Not sure what that means. Also the color green around him. See a huge heartache. Tears. Someone just said he was a great kisser. Old soul.... I am hearing him say he is sorry..."I am so sorry for leaving"...needing validation that all is okay.*

Validation- I'm the great kisser, he used to always tell me I was the best kisser he had ever kissed. My kisses were addicting

Clara- *On his chest he is showing me a woman (tall, slender in build, long hair, full of light) helping a lost soul (male, I feel he is so lost in his transgressions alcoholic, depression) this male has a young child a little girl about 4-6 years of age to live for. On his left side He is showing me an older couple embracing almost like they are dancing happily together, and three children being watched over by an eagle, but when it lands it's an owl. Oddly I can see the eagle and the owl wearing a hanging feather like a small head dress. He is now showing me a playful wolf which is leading me to a tribe. Seeing various teepees, a woman holding a baby is sitting in a circle, she has a brownish red feather facing up on her headdress. It is winter and I can feel and hear the wind blowing, they are near a small thick of trees and on the inner part of some hills. The sun is barely shining over and it makes the snow glisten. Finding it odd that the woman is holding up a naked baby boy. But the sun shines on the baby and leaves a small mark like a paw print on its left side kinda right above the buttocks but to the side. Now the baby is now about 3 and is in the same location but wearing dark brown pants (hide) and a coat that is of white and black colored fur. He is wearing a similar feather as his mom but it is down and to the side. He smiles and waves. He points to a deer. (Thank you for allowing me to read him) very detailed in what he wishes to show people. You may not be tall Hun, but your spirit is big. I felt so much peace there seeing what I was shown. The woman* helping the man crossover may be just a glimpse of what you will be doing and dealing more in detail with, two things come to mind in regards to the little girl. Perhaps the man that you helped pass had a daughter that he didn't know about (she is guiding him) or perhaps your hubby's daughter will be with gift. You're quite welcome Hun. He is an awesome guide.

Validation- What was being shown here is a past life. But also the animals that are in my team. Wolf is very important to me as is the Owl and Eagle.

Kayte.- *I'm sitting at my desk trying to do my work but.......hahaha I'm feeling compelled because I keep sensing and hearing inwardly the following dialogue: Doesn't want to dwell on passing. What's done is done -move on. It's all cool. Now let's get to work. I'm still here babe. I'm not goin' anywhere. Does this make sense? I get the impression that there were people who maybe he shouldn't have associated with but thing is he was a good guy and actually was a good influence and it was part of his path. Goodness my heart is racing as I type. I keep hearing an R name hard sounding. Was there ever a connection to Native rituals specifically centering on bears or shamans? I really don't know why I keep wanting to relate that to the both of you.*

Validation- From the rest of the book so far you can understand this message. I believe that he was talking about my friend Melodie who is shaman and has a bear guide. How we are connected. Also how to move on with his passing and my guilt. Can't change the past. Many bad influences crept into his life.

Libby- *I feel like he did really love your cooking and I feel him telling me you were always mothering him.Which I feel he also loved but not always. The reason I see soup I think is because it's a comfort food. He was very gentle though I feel. He says Angels and I see them but he makes it sound like you talk to Angels. I also feel you've maybe seen him I feel like he's telling me that. Do you still have his T-shirt? He told me to ask about a T-shirt. I feel like he comes and goes. Between there and somewhere. I'm so sorry for your loss...Thank you and thank him for the opportunity to read this wonderful man. He was like jumping around so energetic like he was excited the clothes told me you had all of them...I think he said under the bed so funny...*

Validation- He loved it when I cooked. Was always complimenting me on food. I do talk to Angel and have quite the connection to them. I do have a shirt of his. He did and does come between here and there. I have his clothes under my bed. Can't bring myself to wash them, they were his work clothes.

Treacy-*The first words I heard looking at this picture were: "experimental", "exploration", and "confusion". I feel this person dealt with some emptiness feeling lost and non-connected to those around him at times. Kind-hearted (I heard twice, one time he described himself to me as such). He was sociable, but I definitely felt there were barriers he put up because he did feel alone even when with others. He was blessed with artistry in his perspective of things which he may not have even been aware of himself. His personality really seemed have characteristics of both male and female...for example: strong yet quite gentle, guarded yet inviting. He was compassionate and had a "dancer's body" is what I heard. He seemed to have a hidden side; "not an open book" is what I heard. I am hearing an M name associated with him (Michael, Marcus, Mark???) I am seeing something metal around him. I feel his passing was accidental. He told me, "Something happened to me that was wrong. They did something that was wrong." He also told me, "People say I was one way, but they didn't know me." Thanks for the opportunity to read, Wolf Spirit. Thank you, Spirit, angels and guides. Thank you, kind person for allowing me to connect with you.*

Validation- Basically everything she says here is true. I believe that a lot of it was what she said in the beginning. He used to say that I was the only one that truly knew him. He showed me a side he didn't show anyone else. He was kind hearted when he was sober. He did put up barriers even with me for a long time in fear. He was very artistic and liked to draw things for me. He was very sociable at times and guarded at others. He could be gentle, only when he was himself. He did have female and male qualities like she explained. What's funny about the dancer's body? Yes he did. But there was a time after his passing that I went to see Chippendales dance...There was this guy there that reminded me of him completely. Something about him. HIs body everything. Even had the long hair up. Spirit can sometimes come into peoples bodies to present themselves in that way or send people as reminders. I feel this was his way of dancing with and for me so to speak. I just knew it was him, which is really hard to explain This was his way of validating that to me. The M name could be my Grandmother, or my Uncle Michael, I also dated a Mark. I always sor of felt there was something iffy with his passing other than I know he chose to leave his body at that moment.

August 23, 2014
There was a loud knock in the kitchen

August 24, 2014
Another Knock in the kitchen

September 3, 2014
Found 2 feathers in odd places. Saw a Cowboys sticker on the back of a car (which Rocky loved cowboys) Saw 33, 3 different times and there was a license plate that said 6RNR9. 6 is our anniversary day, RNR love and 9 is his birthday month. Or could be viewed as 69 in a dirty way which is how his mind went sometimes but also today is 9/3 Opened the computer and it was 143. (I Love you)

September 8, 2014- Happy Birthday Rocky

Happy Birthday my darling. I remember your first birthday with me. I sang to u in a Marilyn Monroe voice and it was one of the most beautiful things anyone had ever done for you. That moment will replay in my mind and I will always remember it. .Today I celebrate you and all you are to me. You still do so much for me and others tha are connected to me. You are a gift to every life you had ever touche and continue to touch. I love you from the very depths of my soul and beyond. Going to bake you a cake today, wanted to release balloons but they are not floating anymore. Know that because of today in this lifetime you were able to be a part of my existence Miss u every day. HAPPY BIRTHDAY!!

This day I had an event opened on Facebook and so many people gave their love and thanked him for bringing all of us together. It shows that we are doing our work. The dark was able to stop us and they never will.

September 22, 2014
Dog was barking at the corner where the bathroom is.

September 23, 2014
This doesn't have anything to do with Rocky but is a dream about this soul mate man that is supposed to enter. So I planned this wedding before I even met this man because my guides had told me I needed to plan it before we met and I would meet him on the beach. I was stressing out because I had not met him yet and people were showing up and this person in the dream made me a humongous cake. At the end of the dream I go on the beach and my soul mate is there ...and he comes up to me and says that his guides told him the same thing. I feel like this was a meeting between us in the dream world

September 24, 2014
A bird landed on the screen. I never have birds land on the screen

October 5, 2014
Elijah and I went to a pow wow. They have a campground where you can stay the night. I found a penny in the dirt and the year was 2012. The year Rocky passed. Saw a butterfly.

October 6, 2014
Our 3 year 3 month anniversary. I got up and saw 7:11 on the clock. This is the month and year we got together

October 11, 2014- Shamanic Exercise Upper World
I found myself walking on a beach. I always see myself as this beautiful woman with long wavy dark hair and a beautiful face in a white gown. There was a tall tree with branches reaching into the sky so far that they disappeared into the clouds. On the tree trunk there were little steps. I climbed those steps to the branches and walked them up into the clouds where I pushed through what felt like a

membrane. It then lead me to the top of the clouds. Waiting for me was my Twin Flame and Guide Rocky. He told me he was glad I was there. He took my hand and led me through a light... on the other side of the light was a beautiful garden. There was a bench and there were beautiful roses and lilies. One of my guides walked up it was Maya she said "welcome dear one." Her hair was braided on each side and as always she looked like a beautiful native woman. Then I saw my father from a Viking past life Alvis and he was big and strong very much resembles my twin flame in his face structure but has long blonde hair and blonde facial hair. In the background stood another lady with her hair in a ponytail. She looks myan. Then there was an ancestor, it's the same one I've been seeing. He has a big feather head dress like the chiefs wear. I saw a Monk he was in a brown gown and bald, older. I saw 4 Angels...One was AA Jeremial. He was stunning with beautiful blonde hair and a handsome elf like face. AA Michael was there as well with all of his dark features. AA Gabriel was there, beautiful as ever. I also met my Guardian Angel. He had long flowing dark hair. I shook my guides hands and said I was thankful to them and happy to be there...(during this time I could feel tingles on the top of my head) They said this was only a little bit of my spirit team that I had a few more and also ancestors that help. My Twin Flame looked at me and said "it's time to go now Baby girl. "He took my hand, walked me through the light and we were surrounded by clouds. It was beautiful. He took both of my hands in his and gave me a passionate kiss goodbye. I walked back through the clouds, through the membrane, down the tree and back to the beach...

October 12, 2014-Shamanic Journey day of Ordination
I went to my beach and through a tunnel in the ocean, walked through the white light. I was met by Anslow, Orakle, Snake and Unicorn. They showed me healing people with my hands and shaman ways, ordaining marriages, .counseling people...they showed me many many people and said, "These are the people you have helped and the people you will help. You are to bring light to this world and help

by healing people's mind, body and soul. This is what you are meant for in this lifetime." They kept showing me these images and telling me what I was meant to do. I said, "Goodbye" to my guides and went back through the white light, tunnel and I was back on the beach. I took a moment and looked up at the sky, put my arms out and took a deep breath.

October 13, 2014
Smelt cigarette smoke and the Christmas lights that hang year round for lighting were flashing.
Rocky was a smoker so was Grandma

October 17, 2014- What I learned in a Journey with a Spiritual Teacher

 I learned that I need to talk to my anger and sadness and resentment, get to know them then release them. I need to let go of the fear that this new relationship in the future will be like the others. The pain in the back of my head that I had been having is cell memory and also heard consciousness. It comes on at times because I was punished for speaking out and for being psychic. I need to learn that it's ok to be psychic I will not be punished in this lifetime. Anslow will work with me and controlling the energy so I don't get a headache when I channel. The woman that I see is me with the beautiful long hair; it's what my spirit/soul looks like. It's who I truly am and she represents beauty, gentleness and grace. It's time to learn to be gentle with myself but also these things represent me. It is the goddess like energy in me.

October 19, 2014- Shamanic Journey to the Lower World
My intention was to see the lower world and my guides. I walked along a beach and came upon a cave. I went into the cave and there were native writings on the wall. The cave went down into the earth and I followed it. I walked through the light at the end and it lead into a jungle like place. There were flowers but lots of green, sights and

sounds of a jungle. My Wolf Anslow was there. I met him. Also my big bright green boa slithered up to say "hi." My Eagle Orakle was on a branch overlooking us and then I met one I have never met before. A Beautiful white unicorn. I walked up to him and touched his nose...he was magnificent! I continued down into the forest a bit just to see. It was so beautiful with green lush trees and plants. I turned around and decided to come back. I said "Good bye" to each of my guides. Orakle came off the branch onto the floor so I could touch him. I touched his breast and I said "goodbye" the unicorn by touching him as well. I whispered so long to my snake by petting his head and by to Anslow by petting him and kissing is nose like I always do. I turned around and went through the white light back under the ground and walked into the cave where I saw the native writings again. I ended up back on the beach.

October 22, 2014

Was in a lot of pain so I went to the hospital to make sure everything was ok. Felt like I had herniated another disc or something. While I was in the waiting room I heard the name Rocky over the intercom. Melodie told me later that he was there lightly rubbing my back. Certain parts of love songs kept playing. When I got home and looked at the clock it was 333

October 26, 2014- Reading from Tina

"I see the color red. You and him talked about your journey I feel. Is the number 9 important to you? I feel whatever it was he said his time. No worries babe. Like the movie ghost is how connected you two are. Did yall talk about having a boy? I feel a boy for some reason. Do you get signs from him? The color red of course he says. I see bird. Do you hear your name ever called? He says don't worry about the things you cannot control. He is showing me a yellow rose with red in it. He says you two will meet again. I feel you will remarry and have a little girl and possibly another boy. It's going to happen. When you least expect it. Like bam. What is with a wolf? Figurine"

Validation:

In this reading she validates my name being called. Color Red is his favorite color it symbolizes his Native heritage. Nine is birthday month. He sends me birds all the time. Wolves are my heart As we know by now I have a wolf guide.

October 28, 2014

The fire alarm went off when Eli was getting ready for school as if to say "Hello Eli." He used to always help get my son ready for school. An idea popped in my head for a show and book that may come in the future. I then realized that I was supposed to call for Jury duty. I feel he was helping me to remember and realize a few things.

Journey- Saving the child

I walked up to myself and asked her what I could do. She said "spread love, Love yourself, give love and receive love. Also let go of the anger, sadness inside of you. All of your trials and tribulations have made u who you are this life that and this remarkable, own it! realize it's all in your past and heal from the wounds done to you. Know that a better future lies ahead but u need to release the pain and the hurt. I realize you have many scars, they will always be there, but heal your soul a bit, retrieve it. I told her I would do as she asked. I hugged her tightly told her I loved her. Her head was at my chest and my hand touched the back of her head. She then turned into a mist and went inside of me. Now we are one.

October 30, 2014

Rocky has been telling me to quit stressing....Driving I saw a heart cloud and I had a feeling to bring my camera before I left but didn't. I hate when I don't listen to myself. I was singing in the car and when I was done I heard Rocky say "That was beautiful baby girl you sing like an Angel" He made me giggle. I stopped by Carls Jr for a little something and the to-go number was 22. (This is a twin flame number that means your twin is watching out for you on the other side) I went to the Dept. of Motor Vehicles and they gave me a temporary registration the number was 11. Then when I got to the car I called the office of the CHP that gave me the fix it ticket to explain to them that I still needed to get my car to pass smog but the registration was paid...they said I could take it to the CHP and they would sign off on it if I'm taking the steps I need to. After I hung up I heard Rocky tell me..."See baby girl I told u not to worry about it" then a van pulls in next to me the License plate says 333. I started Laughing...and said "OK Rocky I get it" lol So I go to the place that I was sent to for Electrical and I pull in and the car in front of me license plate has a 33 on the end. Turns out the guy knew what he was doing. He pulled out my radio and then plugged in the gadget to see if it would read, and it did. He said after I get it to pass smog to bring it back, then he fixed my headlights. Until now I only had brights. I had been told it was electrical. He ordered the light bulbs they came right away and he put them in and it worked. I asked him how much for the light bulbs and he showed me the bill it was $15. So all I had was my card and I gave it to him. He said his card machine wasn't working. I said "I'll go get cash" he said "don't worry about it." I went to walmart and got back in my car at exactly 1:11. I went to the GI Dr. I'm in the waiting room and I see a vision of Rocky sitting next to me with with his legs crossed like he used to sit in those damn checkered shorts and long socks looking at a magazine and he said "I'm in the dry with u just like I always used to be" I leave the dr. office and there is a man outside with a 33 on his shirt...Next time I look at the clock it's 333.

November 4, 2014- Rocky and I's 3 year Wedding Anniversary
I miss you like the flowers miss the sunshine on a cold winter's day
And that missing you will never go away
But in my heart you will always stay
Memories etched into my mind
How I long to hear your voice one more time
On this journey of my soul's path
I feel you leading me to the green grass
You guide me to my divine plan
Because of you I am strong
And my walk in the light began
Knowing you are by my side
Throughout all the times I cried
You always said written in the stars we are meant to be
For all eternity
I look up in the sky

And feel you close by
There are times I feel the bitter cold
Wishing you were here to hold
Then I feel a brush of warmth
And realize it's your spirit coming forth
Sometimes I wish I could just pick up the phone
To know I am not alone
So many signs I see
From you to me
I know you are happy now
And forever we will have our vow
Our love is deeper than the ocean
And forever it will remain
Because our souls are the same

Happy 3 yr. Wedding Anniversary Rocky

November 11, 2014
I was watching a movie and right when he calls her and says "hey babe" the movie stops and goes to the fast forward and rewind screen. The Wii remote was on the coffee table and no one was around it. I said, "Hey Rocky very funny!"

December 15, 2014
I'm thinking we just had spirit in the house!! But I feel it was to hear an owl. Because the internet it shut off the TV because we were watching Netflix and our internet reset itself. However, our lamp and X-mas lights flashed 3 times (there's the number 3) and during the silence we heard two owls! I tried to see them outside but can't find them and there was really no wind it was still when I stepped outside. I've been asking for big signs. I honestly don't see or hear them around here. When the movie reset it said Rocky Mountains. When I hear the hoot of an Owl it just really touches my spirit.

Owls can announce the spirit of a family member. I also feel like this was mine and Elijah's Owl's coming forth. Since this experience we have since learned we both have them as guides. Owls are about Clairvoyance, prophecy, Intuition, and seeing the darkness in people or what is hidden. They are also in tune with the moon and the night. Owls can also signify transition. With Owl totem you may be able to see better in the dark and don't like bright lights. I can definitely relate to all of this. (Since this entry we had two more owls hooting outside very loud afterwards I was given visions of prophecy, and some of what I had seem came true)

December 25, 2014
Astral sex again...Amazing. What a beautiful Christmas present. And yes it was him. I saw him, felt him. Twin flames can have this.

January 7, 2015
Melodies and I were talking, she told me to feel behind me that Rocky was there. I did and my hand was on fire with energy. It was an amazing feeling. Just beautiful and he was giving me healing in my crown chakra.

Melodie- *"True love is that. I knew you would be unblocked and spirit would let you know when in a special way. When I get unblocked it's always with something beautiful. That's why yesterday I pushed u to go away and spend time with him. Coz they don't just come for a minute I've had spirit ppl spend hours with me and I use their energy for whatever I need. I sensed it was to be a private moment for u and him too so I knew to let u go. I'm over the moon he's with you. It helps heal you and maintain that loving connection. Well twin flames have been around since beginning of time they just didn't call it back then. It's a soul contract and as u know reappears in several lifetimes over and over. I've had some elders talk to me of it but they see it a bit differently to how you see it all over Facebook and stuff. Like modernism kind of trophies it. Elders told me TF is kind of like a tattoo marking. Spirit targets you and watches how you proceed with it. What you learn from it. How you use it. Like they described it more as soul binding. "*

January 11, 2015
Saw a license plate that said RNR. Then all radio stations had commercials except for country and the song playing was she's everything.

January 15, 2015- Past life Journey
The first life I stepped into was one that Rocky has showed me before. I was a squaw/native American woman. I had 3 kids, one my son Elijah, one was Dove (who I miscarried in this present life), and a girl my daughter that I know is coming back this life. They were all beautiful. Rocky rode up to me his face covered in war paint, he jumped off his horse and kissed me passionately. In this lifetime I lost him, he was killed. I felt the tragedy of his passing. The next lifetime I

step into I am a man. A hunter with a bow. I look at myself and I my hands are that of a man. I was handsome though. I have a white horse. Rocky was my wife. I was killed and he held me as I passed. I could literally feel the pain in my chest and the sadness of leaving her. Last lifetime I am shown in this journey. I am a Native woman again but this time I'm a shaman or medicine woman. I'm healing people. It is nighttime and the tribe around a fire. I am healing those that step forward and wish to be healed. Later, I am sitting with the elders inside a teepee.

January 19, 2015
There was a Penny on the floor with a ray of sunshine shining over it as if to bring my attention to where it was. There were tingles on my head and my phone shut off and on by itself.

January 20, 2015- Reading from Rona
"Passed possibly by accident. He loved you very much. He said your group has helped many people. He was easy going and was important for him to be stress free because he was easy going. Regrets not having had time for kids with you. When you are ready wants you to find love. He sits in a chair next to you on the house. Feeling like he loved music a lot. Was trying to see if I got anything else and feels like he said you will have children with the new love in your life. Rocky will approve and bless this Union when the time is right. The miscarriage, boy, is with him. Although you two will always be connected, you will build a strong bond with the new person."

January 25, 2015
Was driving to Bakersfield. The first song that was playing when I got in the car was "You don't know you're beautiful" This was what Rocky used to say to me all the time. That I didn't know how beautiful I truly was. Then "Starlight" came on and I saw Rocky in my mind with his shirt off and hair down in the shower. Then a car pulled in front of me that had 33 on the license plate. "Dark horse" began to play and I saw Rocky and I dancing sexy and singing to each other. Then I felt him touch my face and was surrounded by his presence.

Reading from Ellie-

I see a beautiful blue sky. A sky blue with beautiful fluffy clouds and I see the water. I also see a boat...not big but more mid-size. I feel that this man liked to have a drink or two... He speaks of music and beautiful love songs as in a serenade. I also see the month of August and not sure how you connect with that month. I also see the month of April. A great sense of humor but a most serious side too. I hear troubled angel. As though he was troubled, but also feel that trouble followed him. He speaks of being laid back and observant. He also speaks of the color white...this color to me feels angelic. I hear the lyrics "love is in the air, everywhere you turn around, love is in the air with each and every sound..." I may not be spot on with these words but I feel that love totally surrounds you Rachelle Lapham both thru the work that you do but also with those in the spirit world, surround you with love and magic, support and guidance. As I see a thumbs up from this man. He is your guiding light, your angel. I also need to ask if this man knew karate or a form of training that he would do these movements that were like tai chi...that is the way it looks to me. Struggled to identify the movements.

Validation: I always look at the clouds and see so much in them sometimes. I love the ocean and he promised me one day he would take me to the beach I believe that is where the house is that he has built for us on the other side. Also as stated before, the ocean is where I spread his ashes. He was the perfect size; my head was to his chest we fit like two puzzle pieces. He was built the way a native is supposed to be is what I hear from him. This is something that he would totally say. He liked to have more than a drink or to and that is what caused most of his problems. We did have many songs together and when I hear them I know they are from him in some way, even songs we didn't have together that fit us I feel he brings to me. August is the month that we first met in person, but it's also my grandma's bday. Not sure about April per say...but I think there may have been some really good times in April. He had an amazing sense of humor but at times very serious when it mattered. We made each other laugh all the time. .He was very much a troubled angel...and yes trouble followed him...i'd like to say in the form of people they couldn't stand to see him doing well they had to intervene and take him off track. He is a guide so most likely why the white. I do know that I am very much surrounded with love. I see and feel it every day, also in tingles and chills often. The thumbs up means he is proud of our achievements. He is my guiding light. He actually was a kick boxer...and really good from what he told me. He was trying to get back into it for a while before he passed. He thought it would get him on the straight and narrow and bring in some money. We had a hard time trying to figure out how to get him back in. I know he always wanted to show me tapes; it was something he was proud of. Also, Eli is in karate so it could be for both as sometimes things that come through are.

January 30, 2015
I had received these "Hello from Heaven" cards from a friend. SO I decided to draw a few. What they said matched exactly what I feel he would say to me. I had always worried if he felt pain in the accident and I could still see in my thoughts what I imagined happened. I also held a lot of guilt. Every time a bad memory came in I would try to replace it with a good one, because that is what I wanted to remember. It said "You are never alone; believe in yourself you can do it. My death was painless, please don't worry or hold onto guilt. I am just a thought away. Now I have no pain, I am much better now. Remember me by the happy memories we created. I am here helping you. I watch over you every day. As a soul I can be in several places at once. It is beautiful where I am. I was met by so many loving people. I am not dead. I have a new understanding. I have become one of your guides. I had to leave that way I wish I had told you more often how much I love you.

February 1, 2015

Was having a rough day and was upset about something. Eli was sweet he said "Mom I love you, you still have me, sorry you're having a tough time." Well needless to say we decided to spend a day at the creek. It was a bit of a drive but was felt it was Rocky's' idea, as he popped in my head. So we went. .Talk about the signs! On the way we passed this truck that had 33. I had my 33 jersey on. Then the radio was out until my song came on from him. It was the only song I could hear. Then I kept thinking I was lost and he kept saying "It's coming up." Which of course he was right. When we finally arrive there is an R&R carved in the tree. I decided to give a tree healing because of all the carvings. I felt the energy go through me into the tree and the tree give me energy back but then I put my head to the tree and got a sharp pain. I believe I was feeling its pain. Walking back we saw a heart cloud... (Figures I left my camera at home).   On our way home we saw a huge angel cloud. It was a beautiful day and I felt a lot of spirit with me, including elemental spirits. Happy we decided to go because it put my mind and heart at ease. Was a nice day out!

February 2, 2015

I had a dream of Rocky. Before I went to sleep I told him I was sorry that I forgot our anniversary on the 4th because I have been so busy. And I said Happy Anniversary because it was 3am. I asked him to come in my dream.

He finally did. We were in this house I lived there with other people. He just got out of prison but was so lovely. We would lay and kiss and just adore each other. An ex of mine showed up and I would tell him "Rocky was my husband and to leave me alone" Rocky became protective of me and just looked like he did when he was alive. It honestly was a beautiful dream because I could sense his presence and feel his love.

February 22, 2015- Reading from Violet

"I keep seeing a dark headed man. I keep seeing his back; He's built He loves back rubs. I'm tingling all over. He wants you to stop worrying you are doing great.

Roses. ID but I'm overwhelmed with love for you. I'm crying. You helped him so much get out of a bad place e in life Ty lover. Just a sec I'm overwhelmed. I hate asking this but did he have a drinking or drug problem. He admits to both. OK he's laughing. You knew me babe you brought out the best in me you do everyone. You're the best mom ever. He's saying he needed a mother like you. He's so sweet. He says he has seen all the tears you've shed. I was holding you most of the time. You have given your all from the moment we met. I love the way you sound when you laugh. Don't cry baby. He is full of peace, love and everything. He visits a lot he keeps telling me you were the only one. He apologizes for something. He says you stuck by him no matter what. He drops his head so that means remorse to me. He turned away. Well he loooooves you."

On another day she messaged me saying this- Rocky's pic just popped up on my phone

Validation- Just needed to validate a few things. I believe what he was apologizing for after saying I was the only one is because of when he told me he cheated on me the night that I all that happened. I feel he was apologizing for saying that but also for all that he did to me.

March 14, 2015
Heart cloud

March 15, 2015
Came home to a candle I made on the floor and taken out of the box. No one was here. It was confirmed later by a friend that it was Rocky.

March 20, 2015
Decided to keep the candle that Rocky put on the floor for me. I was told it was a gift from him
So although it would be good to sell it. He said "it's a gift because I needed candles anyway." So thank you Rocky.

Also during a drumming circle for Spring Equinox. The moment I beat the drums I went into a journey right away. I found myself in a Native village. My hair was in braids and I was wearing leather. Rocky met me and took my hand in his. He walked me over to a Palomino Horse. (I have always been in love with Palomino's since I was a child) I think this one was from a past life. I believe I have a connection to one and that one day he will come back to me. I was then led into a larger tent where I met with a Shaman/Medicine man. My head was anointed and I was laid down. Sage and herbs were smudged over me. I became aware of others drumming in a circle around me in the tent. I was told to set up I had been blessed. He kissed my cheek and I was walked out of the tent to where Rocky met me and kissed me goodbye

March 28, 2015
Smelt like Syrup in the kitchen. Rocky always made pancakes for Elijah.

March 30, 2015
Was sitting on the couch watching Merlin with Elijah. The remote was on the coffee table. All of a sudden the TV paused. Elijah just looked at each other and smiled

May 4, 2015
Kept feeling tickles on my arm and face. Almost like an ant but there was no ant.

May 5, 2016
Found feather in candle and took a picture. Rocky's face appeared with blue energy.

May 7, 2015
Heard four knocks on the wall in my bedroom. I was thinking of Rocky at the time of the knocks. His favorite song "I'm sexy and I know it" came on Pandora.

May 12, 2015- Reading
He is very, very proud of his heritage. He is offering me a dream catcher for you. He is telling me that dream catchers are important to

you and you collect them. He is playing music for me, sort of a rap/rock song. He is also playing a native stomp for me. I'm asking how he passed, and he has shown me cancer, but he also showed me a very violent scene. I'm confused with this and trying to reconcile it. It could be that disease was violent to his body. The violent scene must be the crash. I'm not feeling him referencing your grandmother. I sense that his passing has been like a cancer in the lives of those who loved him. I'm feeling such warmth from the love he is showing me that he has for you. He says "yes, your flame, I know I'm hot" hahahahha. lol he knew he was eye candy but he didn't seem to let it run his mind. He's showing me a dream catcher with a heart woven in the center.

That's not the normal dream catcher - that is specifically from him to you. He was fond of drinking, when he showed me the bottle, he was sheepish and hiding his face. He is very sorry for his behavior and asks your forgiveness. He is healthy and whole now, and wishes he had been able to know that feeling better while earthly.

Is it a pungent smell? He is showing me patchouli incense. He is insistent on you having a dream catcher with a heart and hanging it close to your head where you sleep. He wants to visit your dreams more often. You've found feathers. The gray and dark ones are from him. He says white ones are too normal, too common to find. He leaves gray and darker ones for you. Lol this guy likes to stand out! For you at least. He wants you to keep teaching your son "our ways" He isn't telling me, but I sense that it has been a number of years since he passed. Did you ever ride motorcycles together? He is showing me a bike. Freedom. Bikes are symbolic of freedom to me, and to many readers. Ghost Rider in the Sky. He's pulling back now. He's still showing me that dream catcher with the heart. That's really important to him. As much as he showed it to me, I honestly feel that he wants you to make it.

Doesn't matter if it's perfect - it will be beautiful to him and very meaningful between the two of you

Validation- Very proud of his heritage. I do collect dream catchers including the one my side. He did have a violent passing and his passing and things he did in his life were cancer for those who loved him. Mainly me. He shows here that he is ashamed of how he behaved when he drank. He used to spray his letters with Patchouli cologne. It is also a native smell. This incense reminds me of him. I always find the grey and white feathers. He loved that type of mush. Hearts are my favorite shape.

May 23, 2015 - May 24, 2015

Remote kept going to fast forward but the remote wasn't even on. At 4am I was going to sleep and I was shown a vivid image of when we met. I began crying. I said "You were the most beautiful man I had ever seen. Did you feel what I did?" He said "Yes, I was the most beautiful woman in the world, it was love at first sight, but it scared him." Then I was shown the moment we got married. He said "he loved me and had always loved me" I felt as if he was holding me as I drifted off to sleep.

May 26th, 2015

I made an event in Rocky's honor for his third angelversary. These are the replies.

Me: I figured I would throw this event for his 3rd angelversary. This day is a little bit of a challenge for me as it is the same day we met as well. He has helped so many of you find me and there have been many of you mediums who have connected to him. So in those ways you know him. If it wasn't for him I wouldn't have started the grief group. So I wanted to make an event where you could post whatever you wanted to him, weather it was a thank you...or a Hello...ECT....I know he appreciates it!

Eli- *"I love and miss you Rocky. Wish you were here".*

Jan- *"Rocky Lapham it was your Love for Rachelle Lapham and her love for you that brought her into my life! Thank you for bringing her and I together, she is an amazing friend and so sweet and loving, it's* no wonder you loved her so, and vice versa. She is the amazing woman I know because of the love you two share, and through her grief of losing you in this physical world, you both have brought so much peace and love to so many. I am eternally grateful to you, may you be in peace and love, and continue to love and guide Rachelle o her journey, until you meet again. Love You Rachelle Lapham, and I'm always always here for you, so very lucky to call you my friend xoxo"

Julie- "Thanks Rachelle Lapham for teaching me how to mourn the loss of my husband, Rocky Lapham you will forever be missed and loved by the many many lives you touched, rest in the sweetest peace."

ME- "We wanted to take this moment to thank all of you who have been there for Me during the last 3 yrs. Those of you who have lifted me up even just by a hello. Those of you who have cared about our love and saw the beauty in it. Those of you who continue to support me and us. You have all been a blessing in my life.....and we are bot thankful! Rocky I miss the sound of your heart every night as I fell asleep. Although you had many trying times here, your soul has always been beautiful. I am amazed at how much you have evolved while being on the other side. I have learned to slowly move forward with you in my heart knowing that you will guide me every step of the way as you used to always say...."Baby Girl we was written in the stars"....How very true that was & is....Love you Forever and Always.

Violet- "Hello Rocky! I never met you but I love reading about Rachelle 's interactions with you from heaven and I think it's beautiful Love & light"

Diana-"Hi Rocky, I just want to thank you for putting the idea in Rachelle Lapham, your Twin Flames, and mind about starting this group. Without this group I never would have been able to receive m looooong distance call from my son directly from heaven. Please give

110

Rachelle and Eli the strength they will need today and leave them all kinds of signs from you. RIH"

Message from Eve- "*I can't help but feel that was one of the qualities he loved about you so much, coupled with the fact you were oblivious to how incredible you were. That he stood in awe of your light every day and still does. Holding your hand and walking with you through the rain. I feel like he loved you and was very loyal. Like full staunch outer but melty on the inside for the ones he loved. Just a beautiful dude! Ah yeah I know he wasn't perfect... but loved you endlessly that no matter what he had your back. Was he like a wildflower? Cheeky and spunky... can't help but like him... loveable rogue type? Just wants to constantly remind you he loves you... I'm trying not to cry on the train. Lol. You are beautiful. I can see you miss each other very much. Love love love to you both xx No thank you for letting me in a bit on something so special. I think we may have some things in common lol.I know the struggle xxxThinking of you xx thank you so much xx"*

Validation- He used to tell me all the time that he did not know how I could not see how beautiful or incredible I was. I was Oblivious to it. So that was dead on. The rest of it...yes him to a T! The way he feels about me and our love truly touches people to the core.

Michelle-"*Thank you Rocky for helping Erik to find this group of amazing people. So he could communicate with me. I hope Erik is behaving himself, but not likely. Lol"*

Stormee-"*Happy Angelversary Rocky Lapham! Thank you for guiding me and Rachelle Lapham together. She has been a true friend and blessing! Xxxxxx"*

Corrine- "*Thanks Rocky for loving and guiding such an amazing person. You two have been a blessing to so many. Thanks for being a strong spirit, keep up the good work."*

Renee-"*Hi Rocky happy Angelversary, thanks for guiding* Rachelle Lapham *she has been a blessing to me in connecting with my husband and helping me develop my gift... maybe you can help my husband AJ develop his gift so we can connect like u and Rachelle.*"

We also posted songs at this time and I made a couple of videos. This shows that although he had a hard life he has been able to help me touch many people's lives. That is why I wanted to share this with you! Huh funny wrote this at 1:11 not meaning to.

Same day I went into a very vivid journey. Remember, Twin Flames are passionate and intense. Some things have been toned down as it was a bit graphic in a beautiful way. I remember....I was in the bathtub. I put on some shamanic flute music. At first I'm in this native dress made of leather and I look down and see my bare feet. I look almost the same just more tan and native. All of a sudden I am in the middle of all this snow, for miles all you can see is snow and I have warm clothes on with lots of fur. I look beside me and standing there is Rocky in native fur dress as well. We kissed passionately. I watch two wolves run in front of us at accelerated speeds. We look at each other and I tell him "you know I hate snow." He says "yea well I miss it so here we are" I laugh. Next we are in this cave and two wolves sit outside waiting. Rocky makes a fire and calls me to him. He looks at me with this immense love. His hand touches my cheek and looks deep into my eyes. He kisses me passionately and he slowly starts to undress me. Only the sleeves drop down below my shoulder. He kisses down my neck, down my shoulder. I can see the fire bounce off my skin. I do the same with his clothes and kiss down his neck. Down his arm to his chest and kiss where his heart would be. We began to kiss our lips intertwining...I won't go into what happens next but we are two shadows dancing on the wall. I can see a tattoo on his side that matches mine as his body moves. When we are finished we get dressed, sit Indian style and look at each other. He touches my face and tells me how beautiful I am. I just do not know my own beauty. He then talks about how he has seen it all! He watched his whole life review unfold and how much he hurt me. He felt it all vividly and intensely. He felt my heart break. He felt me fall apart. He could see and feel everything he had ever done to me or anyone else. He watched it from his point of view and from ours. He explained that our baby understands and is aware of what happened and why he did not come to earth. He says he knows that when he used to do what he did to me that I knew he wasn't himself. He never touched me or hurt me when he was sober and he never would. Not that it was an excuse but something overtook him that was beyond his control. He said during those moments that it was like he left his body and a demon entered. He said that he wasn't himself during those moments and had no memory. He said the man that will enter will help release in ways that I cannot release myself.   I needed to realize he was also shown all I did for him. He saw how loyal I was...how much I took care of him and all I did for him. From the road trips, when he wasn't home, to when I helped him with his case, all of it! I was more loyal than he could ever have imagined I would be. I was special and not like others but he didn't know that because he had always been hurt by others. He was also blinded by the drugs and alcohol. He saw and felt how truly and deeply I loved him. How he was my everything. How stupid he felt for doing everything he did and not seeing all that was in front of him and choosing me instead of the addictions. He wished he would've been stronger for us. I needed to understand all of this and in the understanding I would find forgiveness and release. He didn't realize at the time how honest and loyal I truly was and he apologizes for it. He was shown all of this and he was in agony over it, which he felt he wholeheartedly deserved. He told me I didn't need to feel guilty when the other man comes along, that I deserve to live a happy physical life and have my daughter back. I deserved to be completely loved without all of the bullshit. He was sending me a man that wouldn't' hurt I and that was beautiful and stronger than he was able to be in the physical. There would be no demons attaching themselves to this new person because this man would be spiritually strong to match me. He would look little like him because he knows my taste. I needed a native man because in order to grow strong with the work that I was born for and walk the spiritual path I needed someone strong. Someone to teach me the old ways. ..I told him I was thankful and I would always love him and talk to him. He would never be replaced as there is nothing that can break a Twin Flame connection. He said he knows I will always love him and he will always love me! He explained that he is building our house for when I am in spirit and my grandmother visits with him in it often. She has forgiven him for what he did, understanding it from a different perspective. He needs me to release and understand that I can't go back and change things; the past is the past that I need to continue to try and heal from it. He wishes he could take it all back and the memories from it but everything was all part of the lessons and he wishes we would have been allowed more good times together in this life. I have witch blood...shaman and druid and I that I need to find it within me. This is another reason I will meet a native man to introduce me around to tribe and their ways. He has met my friends that passed before him. He said he loves me and how that love will always remain no matter what. It's time for a new chapter in my life. It's time for me to be happy and live a happy physical life because it is what I deserve. I don't realize how truly gifted I am and what a good psychic medium I have become because I am humble. I need to realize this so I can do and attract more work. He said "I love you so much baby girl and that will never change I will always love you." I told him I will always love him that would never change either. He said he would be my guide and continue to guide me throughout my life and visit me whenever he could. One day we would be together again. He said "until that sweet day that I needed to enjoy life." He asked me if I wanted to shape shift into wolves. I said "yes" and so we did! We ran out into the snow, met with

Anslow and we all ran and played. We sat and howled at the moon in the distance. Rocky licked me, our noses touched and I came back my body in the physical...

July 21, 2015- Reading from a few people in an Exercise

Ellie-*I hear him speak, "no greater love than ours, darlin"...maybe a song...but no other words coming to me. For some reason seeing number 21.....I see a single tear roll down his cheek and feel an apology to you Rachelle Lapham...as in big mistake...a miscalculation on his part. He also shows me a jersey with a number on it......but a dark jersey with a number on it and I feel that you wear this or it is a keepsake for you...very precious to you. He tells me and I feel completely chilled "I love you honey"...I can feel the love that he feels for you. He also mentions anger...so feel you are angry for his passing - like cheated out of a life with him. But I want to say that this was divine timing and planning...as nothing is by accident or by coincidence...that you realize this but still cannot accept. He makes me feel that we as humans find it so hard to understand the divine plan and destiny of each and every one of us and so we get angry and bitter and the loss of our loved ones. I also feel he is showing me a cat and this cat feels to be in spirit with him. Also being shown 43 as relevant as well. He also shows me his shoulders Rachelle and makes me feel this was one of his most beautiful characteristics and one of the ones you miss the most of his physical presence with you. He tells me "don't try to deny it"...lol...great sense of humor. He tells me that truly he loves you with every bit of his soul...that you are doing so much better now but still the anger and bitterness comes to the surface now and again. Completely understood by him. He gives me the thumbs up...like you got it...He sends beautiful pink hearts to you Rachelle and one gorgeous long stem red rose...perfect in every way with the strongest stem which is his sense of your incredible strength and determination to continue your path and journey in the face of the loss of him. The rose*

115

as simple and beautiful and elegant as you are...He tells me that he appreciates being able to speak thru me...Please know this dear man is so safe and happy in the angelic realm and most of all and last but not least - he is front and center for you and your son...I feel a younger female in connection to him too...He is also the orb that you see Rachelle...I just saw a large beautiful white orb and this is him.. One of the ways of him being present for you. Also just got glimpse of lots of pink around you...pink beautiful energy. I hope this connection resonates for you Rachelle...he is blowing you one single kiss...wow.. I cannot ever say that I have picked up a younger female with him and I was really surprised because I could not ever remember anything about a daughter...so yes, your daughter is with him...that is the connection...Rocky knew you needed to hear from him and so happy could connect to him for you. He has such tremendous amazing love for you that he gives me chills...I am chilled now...so he is amazing...I know how much you miss him and I know how much he would change things if he could...I know that is a tough one because I have never heard spirit ever say that they want to come back to earth but I think there can be some level of regret, not in the way we humans experience it but in Rocky watching your struggles and not being physically here to help. You know they can create anything they please…

Violet G- *"I immediately got 4 words upon looking at the picture: kind, compassionate, loving and honest. He has an old soul, has lived many lifetimes I feel."*

Validation- There is no greater love than the love of a Twin Flame. Regardless of hard the physical incarnation may be. The love stays strong. The number 21 translates to 3. Which is his number that he makes his presence known with. I did buy a jersey that I feel was sent from him. It is a purple one with the number 33 on it. I mean the odds of finding that jersey in my favorite color are really slim. When I walked into kohl's I made a turn and it caught my eye. It was in the front of the rack. I also had kohl's cash at the time so it was free. I was angry at his passing. I was so pissed for so long at him and the fact that I felt cheated out of the life that we wanted together. I had just been talking to him a few nights prior crying telling him how mad I was at him for everything. I do have a cat in spirit. Actually a couple of them. Could be sammy or snowball. The number 43 could be 7 which is the month we got together but is also my favorite number and my life path number. Also 43 translates to love you. He knows roses are the flower that I love the most. But also he used to say a quote about roses to me. I do get a beautiful white orb sometimes In pictures especially around this time. There is one time in particular where Eli and I were taking pictures and this white orb kept moving and was in every picture but in a different spot. He was showing me that my daughter is with him because I told him the story about what happened and that I had regretted it so much. I loved his shoulders one of the things I loved about his body. This was his way of letting me know he had her in his arms. He is a very old soul.

July 31, 2015-August 1, 2015
Dreamed of Rocky but only remember bits and pieces of the dream. I know it was of him and he was loving on me. I woke up feeling happy.

August 16, 2015- August 17, 2015
Dreamed of Rocky only remember bits and pieces. But we were at a fair eating Fro yo. I felt lots of love. Then this basketball team wanted him to play with him. So he did and I watched. Elijah was running around. Then for some reason his son was in the hospital but as a baby and I went to see him. There was lots of kissing and hugs during the dream. I could just feel soo much love. I remember being home with him and the kids playing outside. I just gave him a big hug and kiss. The song "I Wanna Know What Turns You On" was in my head when I woke up. The night before this dream I felt I was being given a message by him.

August 28, 2015- August 29, 2015
117

I had a dream about Rocky. We were making a house together. We had sexy time then he went a bit gangster. Driving back from Bakersfield I heard a song that said "You were there for me when no one else was" I knew he was trying to thank me for that. Then there was a butterfly inside my car and it flew past me. I went to Del taco and they gave me a 22 cent discount. 22's mean that your Twin Flame is watching out for you. The amount was 2:12, my birthday. Then his song always to me "Just the way you are" played and I felt him singing to me.

October 21, 2015- Reading from Melodie
I got shown a plate not sure if it's dinner plate or like one of those display ones.
He kisses u. Puts fingers on your lips first gently to get your attention then kisses u. surely u feel this coz he wants u to feel he does this. He mentioned how we 'twin flame' talk and shakes head as in no and frustrated. It's like he's saying all these psychics have ruined what it's really all about. He is saying it's a private connection and heart to heart and not something to boast about or tell the world. He showed me a man and woman as like props and each has a huge red ribbon coming from their heart. And in the middle the ribbon ties into a bow and joins them. He said twin flames are a gift to each other. That is how simple it is. And too many don't appreciate this. So I asked if like Twin Flame readings is what to do and he said "yes but strip away the paraphernalia and keep it simple and true and what it is about to the core." I think if he were alive he would not call it twin flame he's indicating that puts conditions on it and rules. He said "all twin pairs are so different no website or book can guide correctly for that individual pair."
I feel another dog is coming for Eli down track. A medium solid one maybe honey in color. But will be intelligent and a strong companion for him. He's giving you a rose. White rose actually on long stem. And indicating to stop and smell the roses still and appreciate the small things for you. The next man that you meet, I feel he will be simple when you meet him but underneath is so much depth to him.

And I know u are frustrated in life. You know that phrase 'pulling my hair out'. I got shown that about you like you are frustrated and no solutions are coming. But it's all part of the journey.

Well the scissor/paper/rock thing was repeated so I felt was important to say maybe he's hinting to relax and be playful. The man he showed me you meet is native as we saw and wearing plain white t-shirt when u meet him. Its event but not seems powwow. I got showed holding hands and long walks on beach so you two develop a beautiful intimate relationship.

Yeah he seems agitated about the twin flame thing but I get it coz all over the place the twin flame thing has gone mad and cheapened. The sacred of it has been discarded.

Validation: I can understand where he is coming from about the Twin Flame thing. That is something he would say as he is deeper than most. Truly he now understands the connection in a way he didn't' before. We used to play Rock, Paper Scissors, and games like that. Everything else she said made a ton of since. I was frustrated very much with life. About the man coming we still have yet to see happen, however it does mean that it is ok to love again after physically losing a husband or boyfriend. I believe the plate was because he used to enjoy our dinners and my cooking.

November 7, 2015

So I wasn't feeling too well today thought I may be getting a bladder infection or something and So guidance said drink some cherry juice. It's like cranberry juice, so I did. Then they said to take a salt bath. So first I took a shower then I got in the bath and I did my prayers and spoke to my guides, cleared my chakras. Next thing I know I'm like In heaven. Literally...This kind of walkway looked like it was gold and shiny and as far as I could see was beauty! Buildings and mountains, it was so breathtaking and Rocky was standing there. We embraced and kissed. He took my hand. Next Anslow my wolf came running up and I bent down and gave him some love. I felt his fur in my hands and nuzzled into him. Then I stood up and I was like where am I? And Rocky said "In heaven, your spirit is visiting." Orakle my eagle was circling. Rocky said "put your arm out." So I did, and Orakle landed on it. I stroked him with my other hand and asked him if he was going to help me with my vision. He said, "Yes. "Our foreheads touched and he flew off. Rocky said "you are so attuned to them because you have had a few lives with them, where they led you in physical form, they were not your pets but your friends" Next my son Dove came walking up, he has gotten big and I picked him up and told him how much I loved him and I missed him but I understood why he is here with his dad and that it was ok. I hugged my precious baby with all of the warmth that a mother gives her son. Then my daughter came walking up (I had an abortion yrs. ago, long story) she is big of course because it's been about 9 yrs. and her hair is in braids. I embrace her and ask her if she is coming back soon. She said "yes. Very soon"... I said "ok good because I am ready to have you. I miss you. You and I have always had a connection and I know I will remember you are coming back to me and I hope you do too" we embraced. Next my grandma came walking up. I ran to her and hugged her, I began crying. Meanwhile in the bath there were tears streaming down my cheeks. I told her I loved her and missed her so much and that I was thankful she was here. Then I was surrounded by loved ones. Great grandmas, a guide, the Native American guy that is always around. I turned and Rocky now has no shirt on and his hair is down with a feather in it. He has on native loin cloth. I said "wow you just have to do that to me!" he replied, "Yes because I know you like it. It comes from a few lifetimes we have had together. Always lost each other but you knew me this way. It's why u long for it." Next to him was his black horse. He said "this horse was with me in my lives." Next to me was my palomino that I always see. Rocky said "this is your horse he has been with you since birth, it is why you always wanted a palomino...You have had him in native lives before and so this is why you have always yearned for him." Next thing I know I am led into a circle and surrounded by my loved ones and guides. Anslow is next to me they are surrounding me chanting and praying and I feel filled with light...so much light...and Next came obsidian (my cat that someone stole from me by a girl named Nicole) He is not dead just his spirit is visiting the other side, being a witch's cat it is easy for him to do this. He has been staying in his body to stay strong but this was important. So he walks through the circle to me and I pick him up and nuzzle him and tell him I am coming for him. He says "he knows". I tell him "I am rying my hardest to bring him home." He says "he knows" I tell him I love him and that I am so sorry I allowed her to take him that I was ust scared. He said that he understood why I did what I did and it's not right for her to keep him from me. He says that he pretends to be nice to her so that she won't do anything bad to him. He says he loves me and that he will be home with us in one way or another. It is just taking some time. I give him a big hug and he says he has to go. I say Ok I will see you soon. Next Rocky comes up to me with a feather and he performs a ceremony on me. He writes symbols on me with the feather and then he repeats the same in the back. He takes my hand, my grandma walks up to me and has a ribbon in her hand. I ask her what she is doing and she says that she is going to join me and Rocky. That they notice I listen to Rocky and hear him the best and so he has become my main guide. Although Anslow is still my main animal guide this is a different type of guide. She says "although I will find love again on the earth plane and there will be much healing from it that mine and Rocky souls are connected as he is my Twin Flame and that bond and connection is so strong and that he wants to guide me." She says that the new guy will understand this. She said that by doing this I will become stronger. So she takes the ribbon and it is gold and she wraps our hands. She tells me that Rocky has learned much and is sorry for the way he was in his physical life and that loving me and guiding me from here is what he feels he must do to make up for it. She says that I will work with missing people and I am given visions of me walking in places being guided and looking and that all I need to happen is for me to find one person and then it will be like a domino effect. She says that I will do this because I want to so badly and it is what I am meant to do, that by doing this hand fasting I have gone up a level so to speak. Now I know that me and rocky will always be connected as one. She comes in and we surround her with a hug. Rocky and I share a kiss and embrace as we are lifted up. We are no longer on the ground and everyone around us is praying and changing and sending light. I see all of my animal guides in the back of the people surrounding me. When we are brought down he says that I can do anything I put my mind and intention to and that he will help me. They will all help me. That I am mean to make a difference. I tell everyone thank you, I give rocky a kiss and walk back and I am here, back in the physical. Feeling *refreshed and revived and just feeling blessed about all of this! And it was too vivid to not be real.*

November 10, 2015- Message from Ellie after her messenger popped up and I didn't try to message her and she didn't try to message me. This happened at 2:22 which is a number that signifies twins on the other side are thinking of them, it also means partnerships.

I am hearing that song Ebb Tide...wow and do I have chills! Maybe Rocky wanting me to tell you about that song. He is such an incredible romantic. I know what you were saying; he knows I understand about romance... always a beautiful message for you and such a romantic with music.

"He always steps forward...I think that is why I popped up for you...he knew he could get thru to me and that I would pass along yet another beautiful song to his lovely lady...wow, you were so very lucky to have him. I have never encountered energy from spirit with such heartfelt love. I have had a few that sent chills throughout my body, but Rocky just has such incredible love for you. Yes, he is...happy I could help today and make you feel the love he has for you. He knows he can stop by anytime for me to carry his messages to you. I also want to add an incredible sense of pride and gratitude for the job you are doing with your son. I need to add that too… I feel Rocky knows how hard you are trying. Is this Rocky's child with you? I feel it is. Okay, that I was not sure about...I did not feel a physical connection to your son but definitely a strong bond with your son if that makes sense. I also feel that Rocky was rebellious in many ways...part of the negative side of him. But yes I feel that you and he had this incredible passion in the physical world. I always feel the romance that spirit feels towards their wife or girlfriend. So I feel that Rocky sees himself in your son. That he has some of those rebellious ways which makes mothering a bit difficult too. I may be off on this but it is what I pick up. So I am getting that accurately. He still beams with pride for the job you are doing and you are doing this alone. I feel he feels a bit bad about that. Like he left you to deal with life on your own. So I want to say an apology for

living as he did and passing in the time he did. But he makes me feel you are strong and can see things thru with your deep connection with spirit, you will be guided with the right steps to take along with the support that you need. Spirit - Rocky will never let you down.

Yes, with proper guidance and support your son's abilities will blossom beautifully and Rocky will work with him. Did Rocky kind of slouch back in chairs or on the sofa...kind of like, yes, I am all that and a bag of chips too...haha...I keep seeing him doing this. I am picking Rocky up well. He shows me too beautiful doves flying around your shoulders and head...so pretty. It just occurred to me that doves stay together I believe with their mates. Yes, then I would say very true...He showed me a picture of doves flying around you...not something I usually see. Check it out...so happy Rocky stepped forward to chat today...YAY for Rocky... it's interesting because the songs I hear from Rocky are actually older songs but my mom was a romantic and loved music so I grew up around these beautiful songs. We know that spirit works with our frame of reference and I can actually hear these songs coming from him. It is about working with the medium who can make sense out of what they want to say. That is so sad that you have lost 2 children. I am very certain that Rocky would be taking care of them. Awesome, I love the way Rocky stepped forward and you have been validating exactly what he was saying. I am blown away as I was not expecting to hear him so clearly. I wasn't looking to chat with him."

Validation: Everything that she said was true in the way he presented himself and his feelings for me. The doves in this meant a few different things. First our son's name is dove which I found out in another reading. I always receive dove feathers in the most amazing places. But also there are beautiful meanings of love and peace from dogs. As well as femininity, maternity and prophecy. Doves are associated with many goddesses such as Isis (he used to call me his beautiful goddess). So it is a symbol of the mother. The name Dove is known to be given to oracles and prophets. My son is very gifted on the other side to have been given this name especially because although in spirit he is the son of Twin flames. They also use Dove feathers on prayer sticks. Since we are both into the native way and I began following that part of my soul after he passed. I feel this was also a message about my link to native ways. A Doves cry can signal water is near by and it song speaks to all that will hear it. Its tones stir the inner woes, emotions and internal waters.

November 26, 2015

Dreamed of Rocky. It was kind of weird but one thing I did understand was that he was saying as Twin Flames we would always be connected.

January 4, 2016- Reading from La Rae

"The first thing was the connection with wolf, but that could be from our conversation. Not sure if this is someone who died from a crash, but a crash was the very next thing I saw, along with a slowed heart rate and labored breathing. So much sadness actually. He was intense and sure of what he believed/knew. Not a lot of second guessing with him. As if no one could change his mind. I feel like they say he died instantly but that in fact he didn't die quite as instant. He had enough time to realize he was about to pass. He knew what was happening. He tells me he told you that tho? Cause I see him lying there looking up, and realizing, "ok this is it" Not in pain, but just knew it was happening. His mind was alert enough to know that. Ok, so when you say that tho, you mean he knew it was going to happen? Because that's the part I'm seeing is that he knew when he was done.Ahh, yea... See I think he KNEW you knew tho. He KNEW you sensed that he would be gone at some point. He says, "that's why the anxiety of leaving" But you guys were distant somehow? Physically? He says definitely not mentally or spiritually. He says he knew from the beginning but that maybe there was some fight inside him at first. Denial maybe. Because I get the feeling that he didn't want to hurt you. I truly think he knew his time was short,

somehow. Maybe subconsciously. "He knew he loved you from the beginning and that you guys were one" Was he using needles? Or could just mean a hard drug in general. He shakes his head. I'm not sure if he had a bad mouth lol, but he says "fuck, it pisses me off" As if he let himself down. Lol he thinks your humor is funny... He tells me, "See... She knows" He is disappointed more than anything. Says "the shit is hard to shake" I see him leaning on the side of a wooden type of wall. All "Joe cool" Very certain of himself. He loved you, though he says you don't need to remind her... She knows full and well. He says he knows he fucked up, but is also surprised because he didn't know a relationship could carry on to the other side... Let alone still grow. Says he's grateful for that. He did, he says "baby that kind of struggle is the kind no one can pull you out of, not even love" "Some things are destined" He keeps showing me an Indian style dream catcher..? Do u relate to that? Oh ok. Confirmation. He gives thumbs up with a smirk out of one side of his mouth. Very handsome hehe. Yea, his eyes tell a story that's for sure. He has the eyes that you could look into and see an entire story written out. He shows me his biceps when you say that. He says "I won"... But I ask him how? He said, "In the end, the light always wins no matter what" And "don't worry, we're not done. This life was lost, but not the next" Yes, where you are going is forever after this. Whatever one may believe that to be. He's leaving but just shows me a fire. Well one thing I know for sure is that he is with you often. He loves you. A lot. Happy anniversary"

Validation- Just needed to validate a few things that have not been mentioned yet. Most of this after reading this book so far you can understand hopefully. About the drugs and how it was an inner battle. He was a very Joe cool person. But I think the wooden type of wall is because he used to cut a lot of wood from trees and we had a huge wood pile! I believe what she meant or was getting about the knowing. I felt we both knew he was going to pass on a soul level. I always knew I would lose him physically. Idk how I knew it but I did. It was always a very strong feeling. Every time he would leave I would flip out. He always told me that he knew he would live a short life. I think as time got closer he knew and that is why he began saying "death before I dishonor my wife" The Dream catcher. I have them everywhere, but are you ready for chills on this one? I have a dream catcher Tattoo on my side that I had done in honor of us. It has two wolves on it, the word SHMILY inner-weaved in the web, R&R love on the bottom of the dream catcher, and a teardrop falling from a feather which for natives symbolizes when a wife loses a husband. It is really a beautiful tattoo with so much meaning but it's not quite finished yet. He was the type of person where no one could change his mind. If he wanted to do it he would do it. That's just the way he was. I believe that the fire at the end of the reading was to symbolize the Twin Flame in case you didn't catch onto that!

February 9, 2016- Reading from Kara

"I'm being told by this charming male energy that cannot wait to speak with you hahaha he winks and laughs as well. That explains everything because I kept hearing dad and daddy and I was like ok but you're not presenting as a father energy normally would so that threw me a bit LOL but I did feel a strong love. That explains the very familiar heart centered feeling with you, I must add that he keeps making me feel this heaviness around my heart and chest I hate to ask but does this have something to do with his passing? I feel like he passes in a car accident and chest impact...ok, so yes car accident...but I feel he's addressing anxiety on a deep level from both you and your children, do you have more than one child? He says the youngest and yourself have bouts with anxiety and he is showing you deep slow breaths as things are going to be so great for you, he shows me a silver cord between the two of you and reminds you that you can visit him anytime and that the communication you hear from him is very real...are you doubting the telepathic communications with him? He says don't forget the astral. But Wait; is your son gifted as well and hearing him? It's just a very strong knowing that I have. Tell him he's hearing me correctly he says, never doubt my love. Honey I have to find my charger I'm so

sorry let me find that and finish in going to send this so we don't lose it I've never had this happen in a reading so sorry. He's so adamant about you don't have to miss him because you know where to find him in the astral, he says "baby get in meditation and spread your wings and I'll be right there to lift you up with me" Your son is speaking with him but he says he feels like he's not answering him because it sounds like him (your sons thoughts) He says "you're perfect just the way you are babe"...his energy is very strong as my phone was at 60 when we started. Can I ask if his name started with a J? I'm not certain it's him but I keep hearing John or James? My weak links are names so I apologize if I have this incorrect as I don't feel it's right on target. I'm being told of a new relationship in your life and it's such a blessing for both of you. He says he sees you smile every day and I just love it, he shows me lots of boxes stacked up as if you're moving and talks about him being very happy about the changes you're making and while they are so scary they are going to be fantastic and not to worry so much. I have to ask he's making me feel as if you're moving in with someone or recently have and it's been a scary process for you because you're so independent now. I feel that but I don't feel like it's dead on accurate so maybe he is talking about a move without the relationship but showing tons of cardboard boxes stacked on each other...he's also now showing me a beach and says you two had great memories there. Not all our times were rainbows together but most were and the beach was a special place. I say beach because I see water and a beautiful blue sky, he says he loves you every day to the moon and back and you're never ever alone, ever...you've got this! You're the best mother and woman to ever walk the face of the earth and I was blessed to walk it with you and he sends a wink and a very handsome yet sly grin. I must be honest he shows me you taking the time to lay down and focus on going to where he is so it could be he's telling you how to reach him. It could also be that he's asking your son to speak with him but I did feel rather strongly that he has or is speaking to him but I most certainly can misinterpret the information given .I must say I'm very curious how the boxes will *come into play for you although maybe he was representing a lot of moving and shifting in your life but I'm not one to try to make something stick, it really felt like you bought a home and you were moving from a place that has white kitchen cabinets and a lot of sunlight and I do see a little yellow around the kitchen so keep that tucked in the hat. I am horrible with names I know he's still on me as we speak now saying "ja" I don't feel it starts a J name though I wish I could get it right hahaha he says yes me too! Son? He's saying son? What's your son's name? Or a future person to come for you lol sorry I normally never stay on an issue but he's really on me about the name hahaha. Also honey never doubt yourself now this is me speaking but you are so connected with spirit and your intentions are so pure and as long as you're here to serve its my personal opinion that they will help you do just that! I always say they are right but I may not be. I have had people flat out not take what I gave even when spirit was telling me it was true and I've had others not take it at that time and come back later when they sat with it for a while, bottom line is never ever doubt, spirit will give you exactly what the person needs and that person's higher self will give it to them at exactly the right moment that they will accept what was given. So never doubt, always serve and you get what you have today, you! A beautiful woman whom is very connected to spirit and passes beautiful healing and loving messages to souls whom need help moving forward in life after a loss, be proud sweetie you have great things happening for you. There it is! The Ja -jah! Soon as I read your son's name he yells that the name hahaha oh gosh I could not get that for the life of me! Also the moving could be future as it's difficult to feel the energy of past present future sometimes."*

Validation- I just wanted to validate a few things here. I have been told by many psychic/mediums that I am going to move. I have seen this move myself. So in this reading she may be describing what she sees the new house will look like. Hey maybe this book sale will enable me to do just that! So I can see why he may have brought that through. Also, it could be the many shifts in my life; spirit can be very symbolic with certain things. I do feel this was a future he was telling her and validating what I have seen so many times. My son is very gifted many who believe know he is an indigo child. He has talked to Rocky many times in his head and seen him. We did have very special moments at the beach when he was alive. Those were some good memories. He also used to tell me he was going to take me to the beach, as in moving there. Sometimes things that come through can have double meanings so the boxes could've meant this as well. This was mentioned in earlier chapters but I just wanted to remind you why she was seeing the beach. It was very special to us. I have always connected deeply to it. In a spiritual sense it symbolizes spirit and the physical, sand and water. Both Elijah and I do have anxiety sometimes I think its spirit and sometimes it's just the way we are. Part of being a light being I guess. He comes across as Daddy in the beginning of the reading because I used to call him that. The silver cord is what connects twin flames. Whenever a reading is done with twin flames most people should see that silver cord that connects them. I have always sort of doubted myself just because this is all soo new in a way. But really I have doubted communications with him as well because sometimes I think it's all in my head. But then it's too much like him to not be!

March 5, 2016
Today while driving I felt the strongest tingles on my lower scalp for almost the whole song of "Everything" By life house. These were the strongest tingles I had ever felt. Then after I saw a cloud that was a dragon, it turned into two people facing each other and then into a heart. I felt his presence strongly.

April 5, 2016- Reading from Stephanie

"When I called this man into my energy, I feel he had a bit of an arrogant way about him. He put his nice shoes up on my table. He had a nice smell to him. Always he says. Peace out he says. He is a bit of a daydreamer. He said listen to my hopes and dreams. Then he told me to figure it out. lol. Whisper in my ear- does someone hear this man often? He says that he lived life on the edge. Precious

baby girl. Twins =) Angels among us- I have to wonder if this means
someone tried to help him because I have heard this before. Tell me
no lies. Piece of me missing. Turbulence. Anxiety. Fighting.
Torment...Dangerous substance. More things forgotten. Alleviate my
pain. Pushover. Pile it on me...Dangerous substance again. Wish me
gone. Leave me be. Done. Out. Peace. Bring me home. And
something about his brain."

May 2016
There was two dogs that someone owned. We got to talking and one
named Baby Girl and the other was named Rocky.

June 2, 2016
I was messing with my new phone's talk to text. Eli was saying
something and it nowhere sounded like what was typed. What was
typed was "Love you E" we laughed and I said Wow about the E that
was typed. Rocky always called Eli, little Homie E. Eli started crying
but it was a great moment.
June 2, 2016- Reading with Anniella

"I saw him standing with his hand in his fist with long shorts. I see
him sitting down on a light blue couch he's doing something on a
small square glass table to the right of him; I can't make it out...
Drugs? Packing a bowl? Not sure... He has nice hands... I got a
weird feeling in my stomach and a little anxiety...January any
significance? Did he rap? Or dance? I see him with his hand on
his mouth moving left to right bouncing. I feel he didn't hang w the
best crowd. Was he a little depressed? Yes I feel he had a lot of
things running through his mind but never wanted to admit them,
like you say. He was very sexual? Oh gosh lol. I feel like he was
very insecure at times. I feel that chemistry for sure. I'm blushing
lol He says he wishes he would've shown you more. I feel like he's
just so attracted to you and he would be so passionate about it.
Like hard and would squeeze your hips really tight. I think he was
battling himself mostly. Ok I see his hand again they were really
nice hands. He just wanted to be more for you but felt he never
was going to be. I did feel he liked to be taken care of. Vegas?

Haha. Oh now the radio is saying something about Vegas lol I feel he had a great heart but just a rough life."

Validation: I think I need to only validate a few things. His hands were my favorite. I thought I saw the same kind of hands on someone one time. It reminded me of him. January is my son's birthday. We did have an amazing time in Vegas and I fell asleep in his lap in the car. Woke up and my limbs were asleep. We had a good time except for his weirdness in thinking I was looking at other men. He did rap and dance especially in the car. The rest I think you can tell just from reading the previous chapters.

October 14, 2016- Reading from Danielle

"I am seeing a mountain around this man. Maybe he lived in the mountains, died in the mountains, I'm not sure, but that's what I see. I'm being shown a private funeral or a small funeral service. Someone wasn't welcome there, I feel. He shows me the month of May. He shows me a vehicle accident. He's making me feel like he didn't have much family or that he was removed from a family or left his family. I don't know what exactly it is. His mother is in spirit as well. I feel like his passing almost "ruined" someone's life. Not ruined, but when he was gone....it changed someone dramatically. The number 4 is relevant in some way. If you can validate any of that please let me know. Thanks."

Validation from me- If you have been following along all of this should make sense to you. WE did live in front of a mountain and in the mountains. He used to hike in those mountains all the time. Just to reiterate how numbers make sense. I did have a very small ceremony for him. Number 4 would be our wedding day.

As you can see Rocky found many ways to reach out to me from beyond. Sometimes it was through others that were gifted, sometimes it was through signs and feelings, sometimes it was though my own gifts. No matter what he's always tried to make himself known. To let me know that I am not alone and how much in the light he is now. Many may think that a lot of this is coincidence but I assure you I have learned not to believe in coincidence. We always seem to know when our loved ones are trying to speak to us or let us know they are around. Signs are everywhere we look from our loved ones. Weather we want to realize it or not our loved ones come in many forms. I know that he made me a believer and I can tell you all I want about how it felt and how it was...but until someone experiences it for themselves I don't expect them to fully understand. It's so different when we experience it ourselves. Many people probably wonder by now when he was alive why I stayed. As I've stated before with Twin flames it's as if you don't have a choice, your bond is strong and you are connected. You are a part of the other. I don't blame Rocky for his misfortune and the way he was. After learning how all this works I blame the dark for trying to break us apart. But what they did was just give Rocky a way to be free on the other side. To be healed, to be whole. They gave us more power in the end because he works with me on helping others. He is so beautiful now, full of light, all the darkness lifted. Happier than he could ever be on this earth plane. Together we are a team. These were his lessons and ours together. Was it hard and a roller coaster, yes. I promise you that my son was never in danger, as he wasn't around when things would happen. My son isn't even aware of most of this even though he is in his teens now. Rocky would never hurt him he thought of him as his own child. But when a demon takes someone over do we really blame them? When it comes to drugs and alcohol the dark has control. They use people. They get off on the pain inflicted. That is why sometimes you fail to recognize someone anymore. Why they seem to be gone. When you look in their eyes you see emptiness. I decided to share my story in order to help others understand all of this from a different perspective. A spiritual one. To me it makes more since. I never understood how people can change in the blink of an eye till now. There is more proof out there about how the dark can take someone over than people can ever fathom. There is so much more than meets the eye. There are different dimensions, different earth planes. Much of this life has to do with past lives, in order to learn and grow we have to experience a lot. Much of our lives is about karma and lessons. Finding our soul path again. I hope that maybe in the future I can write something that can better explain how it all works.

Last Chapter- A channel from Rocky

First of all I want to say I am sorry. I am sorry for all of the pain I inflicted on my family and children before I even met my baby girl. I want to apologize to my ex-wife and to my kids for the trials I put them through. I realize now all of the mistakes I made. Know that I do love you. I am always with you. In the breeze, a whisper, in all the ways that you feel me and know that I'm there. I have seen you grow up and have not missed a beat. I am full of light now all of my difficulties gone, pain in my soul lifted. I am full of light and I will continue to watch over you. Know that I have always loved you. Walk with love in your heart and kindness in your soul. Remember the ways I taught you.

To Eli, my little man. I am sorry for any pain that I put you through. The moments when you saw me as not myself. I am thankful for all the time that we got to share with one another. All the memories we made. You are a son to me. I am forever thankful that we were a part of each other's lives. I continue to watch over you as well. Please take care of your mom for me. As you grow into a teenager, be smart in your decisions. Always love with your whole heart and be kind. Be strong even when you feel weak. I am forever walking by your side.

My Baby Girl, know that you are without a doubt the love I had always dreamed about. You are my wife no matter what anyone says. We are married in spirit and in life. Regardless our souls created an epic love story in many lives. Some ended good some not. I know that our time on earth this time was short and difficult. I am sorry for that. I am sorry for every single thing, every single way I hurt you. I know I say it a lot and

I know that you have forgiven me but I really wish it was not a part o
our path and that I could take it back. I really wish I was strong
enough to not allow the dark to win. I tried so hard but I was just
wasn't strong enough. As I always said people would try to come in
between us and they did. Our light was too strong for many to
understand. We are a powerhouse together. It's not allowed. For
your path is a great one. You have no idea the light that you bring
this world alone. The love that you give. It is one thing I always
cherished about you. I know now your loyalty, although I wish I had
known it then. I know now I was so wrong about so much. I know
now that our love, our true love without all the buillshit is real, and is
powerful. Twin flames after all are the special. We are here to light
the way for humanity. We are here to bring light to this world. It was
not possible for me to do it physically but it is possibly for me to do it
spiritually. Together we can bring much peace. You are on the right
path, continue to walk it. I know it has not been easy, I know you
have had struggle after struggle. You felt alone but you were not. I
was always walking beside you, working to make your struggles a
bit easier. As time goes on I know it gets different with us. My
presence isn't as strong because you need to learn how to live your
life. You need to learn how to go on without me. However, in a way I
am still so strong in your life. I decided to give you the go ahead on
this book because I felt that it could help many understand addiction
abuse, Twin flames, how the spirit lives on, evolves and changes.
How we let go of the negative and only bring the positive. I know
that sometimes you flash back to the bad times, and I try to help you
remember only the good. The times when I looked in your eyes and
you felt my love. The times I held you in my arms and you felt safe.
The times of laughter. We may not have had many great times but
the ones we had are memorable. We are memorable and it was time
to have our story told. Many will relate to what you have written.
Many will become to believe. Those that didn't believe I loved you
now know I do. Those that didn't understand quite how certain
things work, now do. This is a stepping stone for you. This is the
beginning of something great. You are meant for greatness and

without me leaving you never would have known that or grown to your potential. You would still be stuck. But I released you. I sacrificed myself so that you could live a better spiritual life. To become who you were always meant to be. I ask people to not be judgmental of me or you. As no one is perfect. We all have our own lessons, hurtles, our own demons. I literally had them and many do. Our own things we gotta get to. But we come out of it stronger. We come out on the other side having learned so much and gaining impeccable strength. We go through things in order to help others who experience the same or similar circumstances. This was part of our journey. We have had many journeys together. Twin Flame stories on the earth plane is always tragic. But through tragedy comes great understanding. It is so beautiful over here. The colors are the most vibrant of vibrant. The beauty is astounding. Everyone lives in peace and harmony. I have built our house on the beach and I am awaiting you. You still have so much work to do. I am sorry you have had to walk this road physically alone, but your grandmother and I have been here all along. Now your grandpa is here and he understands things now. He now sees there is another side. He sees things from a different perspective. Although you feel as though you have let him down. You have not. You have not let any of us down. We see that you are trying. We see that you are trying to follow your path. We ask that people open their hearts and mind to this book...To see beyond reality. It took a lot for us to write, but we did it. Finally after 5 years. There was much you wanted to leave out but I told you to write. I know it may make me look bad but I felt it was important to share. Hopefully people can come from a place of compassion and kindness. Thank you for writing it. Thank you all for reading. Much love from the other side! May wisdom and grace surround you?

No Goodbyes

When I think of what could have been

I watch the leaves change colors

And the water wash on the sand

Memories of me holding your hand

Thoughts of yesterday's gone by

Would make anyone need to cry

It hurts me so

When I think back to when u had to go

Tears on my pillow

Painful cries in the night

Makes it hard to continue to fight

Butterflies surround me

Birds fly by

This is you showing me there is no goodbye

I try to be strong

But have weak moments still

And that's when I feel you hold me

And touch me

Chills and tingles

That makes me see